PUB WALKS
IN
SOUTH DEVON

Laurence Main

Copyright ©, Laurence Main, 1994

All Rights Reserved. No part of this publication may be reproduced, stored in a retrieval system, or transmitted in any form or by any means – electronic, mechanical, photocopying, recording, or otherwise – without prior written permission from the publisher.

Published by Sigma Leisure – an imprint of
Sigma Press, 1 South Oak Lane, Wilmslow, Cheshire SK9 6AR, England.

British Library Cataloguing in Publication Data
A CIP record for this book is available from the British Library.

ISBN: 1-85058-359-5

Typesetting and Design by: Sigma Press, Wilmslow, Cheshire.

Cover picture: The Sir Walter Raleigh, East Budleigh

Printed by: Manchester Free Press

Preface

Devon is the most popular county in England with holidaymakers. It is a place that people return to again and again. It is also a big county, being the third largest in England after North Yorkshire and Cumbria. Uniquely, it can boast two distinctly separate coastlines: north and south. Such is the wealth of good walking country that it needs several books to do it justice. This volume deals with the southern shore, including the tract of land which lies south of Dartmoor (known as South Hams) and the southern section of East Devon.

This is where most of the tourists go and the vast majority of Devon's population lives, taking in Plymouth, Torquay and Exeter. Public transport is better than elsewhere in the county, while campsites and all types of holiday accommodation, including pubs, abound. The visitors are made welcome with real clotted cream (and not that thin old stuff they sell over the border in Cornwall, they'll tell you) and cider. All sorts of theme parks, heritage centres, model railways and other amusements await your custom. This is the English Riviera and you can really go to town. The beaches aren't bad, either. Some, such as at Dawlish, are just a short step from the train. There are plenty of quiet, secluded, coves which can only be known to the walker. The public footpath network is, indeed, the key to the full enjoyment of this area.

The Ordnance Survey Pathfinder maps show walkers where the public footpaths and bridleways are. The relevant numbers are given at the start of each walk. An Outdoor Leisure map (no 2) gives good value for the extremely popular recreation area between Paignton and Salcombe. Many of the paths are now waymarked, while new stiles have sprung up across fences which used to prove obstacles to progress.

The South Devon Coast Path forms part of the South West Coast Path, a national trail of some 594 miles in length between Minehead and

Sandbanks, Poole Harbour. The South Devon section, between Plymouth and Lyme Regis, is reckoned to be about 146 miles long. It makes a fine walk and many of the routes in this book incorporate parts of it. On a sunny day you will seldom find solitude on these. Step inland, however, to discover hidden valleys, woodland, interesting churches and delightful old pubs where time seems to have stood still since the days when Jane Austen pictured her characters in their surroundings.

South Devon is too popular with tourists for its scenic roads and charming old villages to bear, so do your bit by not coming here by car. You will gain the freedom of a surprisingly good public transport system. All of the walks in this book were done from base camps at Slapton and Honiton, using public transport to reach the starts of the walks. Western National's Explorer ticket gave excellent value as a day rover on the buses for only £4 in 1993 (adult - child £2.25, senior citizen £3, family of two adults and two children £10). Even more of a bargain is the seven day Key West ticket, costing £19.80 for an adult in 1993 (£14.30 for a child, £16.50 for a senior citizen and £39.60 for a family of two adults and two children). Whereas the Explorer can be bought when you board a Western National bus, you must purchase your Key West ticket from a Western National Travelcentre or agent or by post from Western National, Laira Bridge, Plymouth, Devon PL4 9LP (send an sae for current prices). Trains are quicker than buses and can be almost as cheap when you use a Devon Rail Rover. A seven day rail rover (covering all of Devon and up the line to Weston-super-Mare) cost only £35 in 1993. You can't travel before 9 am except at weekends. Telephone 0392 433551 for current information or ask at your local railway station. There is also the Paignton & Dartmouth Railway. Telephone 0803 555872 for details of its seasonal steam service. A trip on this line (perhaps behind the famous *Flying Scotsman)* forms part of the famous Round Robin ticket, along with the ferry between Kingswear and Dartmouth, the river cruise up to Totnes and the bus back to Paignton. Taking public transport to the walks can be great fun, especially when you have all the timetables to help you plan your trips. Devon County Council publishes a public transport map with a summary of bus services. Write for a complete set of timetables to Devon County Council, Lucombe House, Topsham Road, Exeter EX2 4QW. The County Council enquiry line (8.30 am to 5 pm from Mondays to Fridays) is 0392 382800. Western National, the principal operator, are on 0752 222666.

Devon Tourist Information Centre's telephone number is 0392 437581/ 79088.

There are TICs in Axminster (0297 34386), Brixham (0804 52861), Budleigh Salterton (0395 45275), Dartmouth (0804 34224), Dawlish (0626 863589), Exeter (0392 265700), Exmouth (0395 263744), Honiton (0404 3716), Kingsbridge (0548 3195), Newton Abbot (0626 67494), Ottery St Mary (0404 813964), Paignton (0803 558383), Plymouth (0752 264849), Salcombe (0548 842736), Seaton (0297 21660), Sidmouth (0395 56441), Teignmouth (0626 779769), Torquay (0803 27428) and Totnes (0803 863168).

Laurence Main

Contents

LOCATION MAP

This area is covered by
'Pub Walks on Dartmoor'
by Laurence Main (Sigma Press)

Cornwall

DEVON

Bere
Ferrers
11

•12
Plym Valley Railway

Totnes•¹³

Plymouth Hoe
14•

¹⁷•Ermington

•15
Bovisand Bay

16
•Yealmpton

19
Dartmouth•

18
Loddiswell

•21
Noss
Mayo

Bantham•²²

Kingsbridge

24
•Slapton

23•

25
Frogmore•

26/Torcross

Salcombe•
27

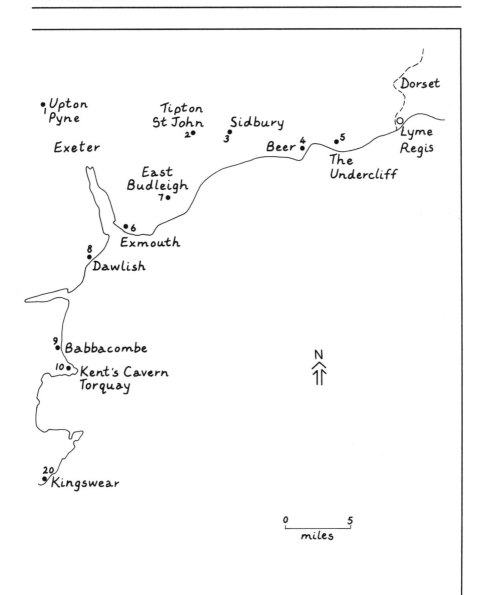

Introduction

Many know Devon from that glorious stretch of railway line between Dawlish and Teignmouth. The famous Red Sandstones are easily seen in the cliffs, indicating the richness of this land. Traditionally, the South Hams district is where animals find winter grazing after a summer spent on Dartmoor. There is more than pasture and cream to South Devon. This is fine arable land, too, favoured by a warm, mild, climate. Cidermaking is a speciality, especially in the east.

The landscape is dissected by a series of river valleys whose steep slopes have encouraged the retention of woodland. The Tamar forms the border with Cornwall before emerging at Plymouth Sound, having come from near the north coast. Other rivers rise in Dartmoor and form deep estuaries or rias which indent the south coast. Chief amongst them are the Avon, Dart, Erme, Plym, Tavey and Teign. Towards the east, the plateau is formed of the younger Cretaceous greensands which are cut into by the beautiful broad valleys of the Axe, the Coly, the Otter and the Sid.

Beer head has the most southerly exposure of chalk in England and there is more chalk along the coast to Dorset. Limestone forms the cliffs and off-shore islands of Torbay, where quarries provide building stones and 'marble'. Other limestone quarries were worked at Plymouth. Agriculture has long been established in South Devon. It has taken thousands of years to build up its patchwork quilt scenery. Modern intensive farming now threatens the diversified wildlife, but there still are traditional hay meadows with ox-eye daisies and a variety of orchids. Butterflies come to sip the nectar of the flowers and to use them as larders for their caterpillars. Look for small copper, marbled white, common blue and meadow brown over traditional grasslands.

Take the bus to the starts of these walks!

Improving the land means grubbing up hedgerows, with the consequent loss of sanctuary for plants and animals. Some hedgerows do survive and are usually a dense layering of hawthorn, blackthorn, beech or hazel. On the bank below are stinging nettles, campion, primroses and wild strawberries. Honeysuckle provides a beautiful scent, while brambles can feed the rambler in late summer with juicy blackberries.

Ancient woodland has survived in patches here and there, while the area to the east of Exeter is blessed with lowland heath. This is characterized by gorse and heathers with some purple moor grass and cotton-grass. Spiders and insects find it a haven, as do all six species of native reptiles. These attract the Dartford warbler, with its rufous chest, blue-grey back and long tail.

Exposed headlands have areas of maritime heath, fringed by clumps of sea campion and thrift. Rarities such as white rock rose and goldilocks aster can be found on the exposed limestone of Berry Head Country Park, near Brixham.

The rivers, which include the Exe, whose source is away in Exmoor, are acidic and flow swiftly. The lack of sediment precludes lush bankside vegetation. Salmon, sea trout, eels and the native brown trout form the bulk of the fish population, although the rivers to the east of Exeter have a more varied population, with roach and dace.

Willow and alder line the banks of the rivers, while dragonflies hover to provide moving targets for swallows, wagtails and, at night, bats. If you are lucky, you may see the blue flash of a kingfisher. There are even a few otters in the rivers of South Devon, although you are more likely to mistake a mink for one.

The estuaries which characterise the coast provide shelter for saltwater creatures. The sea tends to push sediment up the estuaries rather than it being carried down by the rivers. The Exe and the Teign do have mud and sand banks which attract wading birds, however. Look for the elegant black and white avocets during the winter, along with other waders such as turnstone and greenshank. There are enormous numbers of ducks and geese, especially widgeon.

The sand banks, rocks, mud flats and shallows of the estuaries teem with life. Low tide exposes the casts of lugworms, sought by the long, probing bills of the wading birds. Cockles lie just beneath the surface of the sand or gravel. Prawns, blennies, sandeels and small flatfishes survive in the shallows, while kelp hides the sand hoppers. There's plenty of food for the herons, shelduck, gulls and terns. High tides bring other predators – fish such as the bass.

The beaches offer a fascinating study, with limpets, mussels, whelks and winkles living in the rock pools. Shore crabs, velvet swimming crabs and small edible crabs live under stones (which should always be replaced to prevent the creatures which live on their undersides from being exposed to death). Look too for the mermaid's purse, being the egg sac of a ray or dogfish.

All this pales into insignificance when compared with what divers can see under the waves. Basking shark live off plankton, while this is traditionally the area to catch mackerel.

South Devon has a long history of human occupation, from the cavemen of Kent's Cavern at Torquay to the legendary giant of Plymouth Hoe and the Brutus Stone at Totnes. Axmouth, with its ancient harbour and hillfort, marks the south-western end of several prehistoric tracks.

Taking the path back to Ermington (Walk 17)

The Romans made Exeter one of their walled towns (you can still see sections of their wall). The Saxons occupied it by the end of the seventh century, while Guthrum led his Danes into the city in 876 when it appeared that Alfred would prove to be far from great. There is no doubt about the glorious period in the history of this part of Devon. Its chapter was written largely in the 16th century, when some of the most famous names in maritime history hailed from here.

The South Devon ports recorded a thriving trade as early as the 1300s. The trade in wine from Bordeaux became particularly important, with wool going in the opposite direction. Capable sailors soon gained a reputation for privateering. This comprised the licensed operation of armed private ships against an enemy country's merchant vessels. They were, in fact if not in name, pirates.

When the New World and the rest of the globe was being discovered, the seamen of the South Devon ports could hold their own with anybody. Sir Francis Drake was born not too far to the north of Plymouth (near Tavistock). He circumnavigated the globe between 1577 and 1580, then helped defeat the Spanish Armada in 1588. Sir John Hawkins, from Plymouth, also helped defeat the Armada. Sir Walter Raleigh, who was born near East Budleigh (see Walk 7) is another famous hero, believed to have introduced the potato and tobacco to the Old World from the New. His half-brother, Sir Humphrey Gilbert, claimed Newfoundland for England in 1583.

Deep-sea fishing was a parallel enterprise in the western North Atlantic. The islands and headlands of the New England coast, especially in the state of Maine, became the fishermen's land bases. The people of Newfoundland still speak with a Devon accent. When the famous little *Mayflower* arrived in North America with its band of religious enthusiasts, it found itself docking at a place already called Plymouth. *Mayflower* had, of course, set sail from the original Plymouth in Devon, in 1620, having previously called at Dartmouth.

The next great moment in history came when William of Orange was welcomed ashore in Brixham in December, 1688. Thus began the Glorious Revolution upon which so much of our present society is based. The rest of the action took place elsewhere, however. Even during the Napoleonic Wars (and the captured Napoleon would have seen the

Hooe Lake (Walk 15)

Devon shore when his ship anchored off Brixham in 1815, then put into Plymouth Sound), South Devon was where people like Jane Austen came on holiday. Devonport maintained the naval tradition, but the tourists had arrived. When the railway reached Exeter in 1844 (and Plymouth in 1848), the numbers of visitors mushroomed. Too many come along the roads today (and Devon has around 8,000 miles of road, more than any other English county, although much of the network is made up of old, sunken, lanes) but the railway still provides a good service. Few journeys can equal the thrill of travelling beside the sea past those red cliffs at Dawlish.

Real Ale

Global trade has resulted in the strange concept of English people drinking tea from Sri Lanka and coffee from Brazil. Apart from the fact that valuable food-growing land in such poor countries is wasted on growing ridiculous cash-crops (with the cash certainly not going to the local people who do all the hard work but who would be better off if their land were used to grow food for local needs), this has separated us from our history and traditions. England is rich in malting barley and the national drink for thousands of years was ale. Only the brave or those fortunate enough to live near a spring drank water. Ale was safer,

Traditional hand-pumped bitter at The Boringdon Arms, Turnchapel

having been boiled and containing preservatives. Ale in the middle ages was thick, sticky and sweet. Exotic spices may have been included. Hops weren't introduced until around 1400. They added bitterness and flavour and had preservative qualities, but took a long time to catch on in England, after being introduced from Flanders. Henry VIII thought hopped beer was only fit to be drunk by Dutchmen and forbade his brewers to add hops. Nearly all ales contained hops after his reign, however.

The Minerva, Plymouth

Each of the pubs featured in this book serves real ale on draught. This means that the beers are still fermenting when they leave the brewery. This is known as secondary fermentation which took place in the brewer's large brewing vessels. The process continues at a slow pace as the barrels are racked in the pub cellar. Carbon dioxide is produced and escapes through a spile hole. The thirsty walker may receive gravity drawn beer, direct from the barrel, or beer from a hand pump or electric pump attached to the bar. Real ale is free of the carbon dioxide or nitrogen used to force pasteurised (i.e. where the fermentation has been killed off) varieties under pressure out of their kegs. These gassy beers are the only ones that need the glossy adverts. They are shunned by lovers of traditional ales.

Many landlords take a different view, however. Traditional real ale is less easy to keep. Great care has to be taken regarding temperature and cleanliness. The draught beer has a very short 'shelf-life' and it takes skill, acquired from both training and experience, to serve a good pint of real ale.

Opening Hours

Under recent legislation pubs in England can now open for a maximum of 12 hours each day on Mondays to Saturdays (being 11 am to 11 pm) and for six and a half hours on Sundays (being noon to 3 pm and 7 pm to 10.30 pm) unless extensions have been granted by local licensing magistrates. Additionally, a growing number of pubs stay open during Sunday afternoons to serve meals, with which alcohol may then be consumed on the premises.

Most country pubs do not find it in their interest to take full advantage of these 'relaxed' hours and tend to stick to the 'traditional' hours of noon to 3 pm and 6 pm to 11 pm or 7 pm to 11 pm. Check each pub individually.

The Walks

Each walk in this book follows rights of way to which you, as a member of the public, have unrestricted access. These are public footpaths, bridleways and by-ways as well as lanes and roads. When surveyed, all these routes were free of obstructions. If you do find any problems, send full details (including grid references) to the County Surveyor, Devon County Council, Lucombe House, Topsham Road, Exeter EX2 4QW, tel. 0392 382070, the Devon Area Secretary of the Ramblers' Association, Mrs E Linfoot, 14 Blaydon Cottages, Blackborough, Cullompton, Devon EX15 2HJ, tel. 0884 6435 and the Ramblers' Association at 1/5 Wandsworth Road, London SW8 2XX, tel. 071 572 6878.

The walks are numbered in sequence (almost) from north to south and are spread all over South Devon. Make use of the relevant Ordnance Survey maps, as detailed for each walk.

The walks average about five miles in length. Several of them link with other walks in this book to allow longer routes to be done in a day, if desired. Other walks can be linked with the aid of public transport.

The following walks can be linked together:

❑ **Walks 2 (Tipton St John) and 3 (Sidbury)** together give a route of $10^1/_2$ miles.

❑ **Walks 4 (Beer) and 5 (The Undercliff)** can be connected by following the Coast Path through Seaton to make a linear walk of some 13 miles.

❑ **Walks 6 (Exmouth) and 7 (East Budleigh)** can be joined to make a long day's ramble of about 19 miles.

❑ **Walks 9 (Babbacombe) and 10 (Kent's Cavern)** are easily linked to give a 7 mile walk.

❑ **Walks 19 (Dartmouth) and 20 (Kingswear)** may be linked with the aid of the Dartmouth ferry to give a walk of about 11 miles.

❑ **Walks 24 (Slapton) and 26 (Torcross)** join together at the boardwalk (don't miss this highlight – do it twice!) to form a 9 mile walk.

All walks should be within the capabilities of anyone of average fitness. Allow about one hour for every two miles, which should enable short breaks to be made. Do not be surprised by the strenuous nature of some parts of the Coast Path (remember, you may start a climb from sea level). Do remember that the physical landscape can change. Keep to the path and treat it as a privilege to walk across the land.

The Country Code

❏ Guard against all risk of fire.

❏ Fasten all gates.

❏ Keep dogs under proper control.

❏ Avoid damaging fences, hedges and walls.

❏ Keep to paths across farmland.

❏ Leave no litter.

❏ Safeguard water supplies.

❏ Protect wildlife, wild plants and trees.

❏ Go carefully on the country roads.

❏ Respect the life of the countryside.

1. Upton Pyne

Route: Cowley Bridge – Upton Pyne – Woodrow Barton – Cowley Bridge

Distance: 5 miles

Map: O.S. Pathfinder 1314 Exeter

Start: Cowley Bridge Inn (Grid Reference SX 909954)

Access: Buses running past Cowley Bridge include service H from Exeter, no 50 between Crediton and Exeter and no 55 between Tiverton and Exeter

Cowley Bridge Inn (0392 74268)

This old stagecoach inn was rebuilt around 1900. Food and real ale are served. The bar opening hours are 11 am to 2.30 pm and 6 pm to 11 pm on weekdays, noon to 3 pm and 7 pm to 10.30 pm on Sundays.

Upton Pyne Social Club (0392 841825)

This isn't a pub but is the second oldest working men's club in England. Manganese miners relaxed here when the local mine was working in the early 19th century. It is open from 8 pm to 11 pm on weekdays, but you may find it open for a drink and a packet of crisps on Sundays between noon and 2 pm (and from 8 pm to 10.30 pm). It is opposite the Church of Our Lady.

Upton Pyne and Jane Austen

Jane Austen came on holiday to Devon in 1801 and 1802 and fell in love with a man who died shortly after arranging to meet the novelist again. Her suffering is conveyed by her novel *Sense and Sensibility* (published in 1811). Much of this is set in the 'Barton Valley', described as being four miles to the north of Exeter. Jane Austen's 'large and handsome house' is Pynes, where the novelist actually stayed as a guest of the Northcote family for part of a holiday. 'Barton Cottage' is probably Woodrow Barton.

Stand between Upton Pyne's church and social club and you could be back in the time of Jane Austen. Cobbles lead to an old lych gate giving access to the churchyard. This is where Elinor Dashwood and Edward Ferrars were married. Notice the figure of Christ over the door of the church, blessing those who enter. There is a splendid view from the tower, taking in the Raddon Hills. The painting of the Last Supper, hanging behind the altar, was painted by an unknown artist and brought from Italy in 1710. The church was consecrated by Bishop Grandisson (who also built part of Exeter Cathedral) in 1328, although there is a record of a church here in 1283.

Pynes was built around 1720 and bears the hallmarks of Inigo Jones in its graceful symmetry. In the novel, it was inhabited by Sir John and Lady Middleton.

The Cowley Bridge

The Church of Our Lady, Upton Pyne, where Jane Austen located the marriage of Elinor Dashwood and Edward Ferrars in her novel 'Sense and Sensibility'

The Walk

1. Go up Stoke Road to the mini-roundabout and turn right over Cowley bridge, crossing the railway near the junction of the lines from London Paddington to Exeter and from Barnstaple to Exeter. Follow the A377 road across the River Exe to Cowley (there is a pavement for most of the way).

2. Turn right along the road signposted for Upton Pyne, Brampford Speke and Thorverton. Cross the bridge over the River Credy and bear left over a stile to follow the signposted path along a meadow to reach a stile in the railway fence. Cross the railway (the Barnstaple-Exeter line) with care and take the stile in the fence opposite. Cut across the corner of the field to go over another waymarked stile (soon followed by a small footbridge and a second stile) in the hedge on your left. Maintain this direction to a gate in the top left corner of the field to gain access to a road.

3. Turn left along the road. Bear left at a fork to enter Upton Pyne and visit the Church of Our Lady (with Upton Pyne Social Club across the cobbled yard from its lych gate).

4. Walk back from the church to the fork and turn sharply left along the road signposted for Brampford Speke, for a quarter of a mile, until the end of woodland on your right.

5. Turn right through a gate to follow the bridleway past woodland on your right and fields on your left. Continue down this track to pass the farm buildings of Woodrow Barton and descend to a signposted path junction.

6. Turn right along the track with a fence, soon becoming a hedge, on your right and meadows on your left. When it bears left to a weir, take the signposted public footpath ahead through a kissing-gate and along the edge of a wood on your right. Emerge through a gate to walk with a hedge on your right and see Pynes across the field on your right.

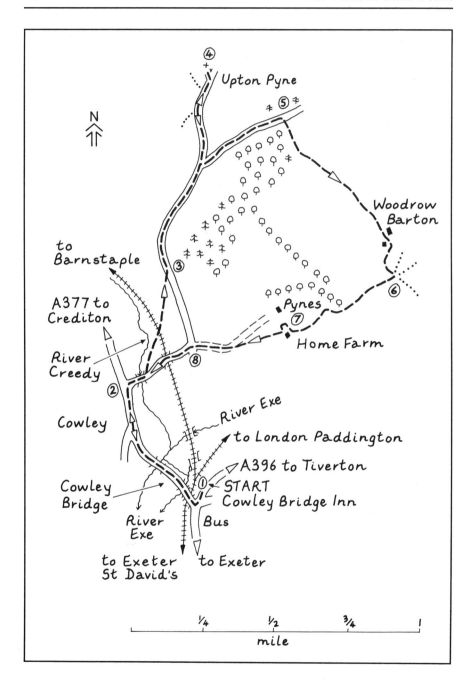

7. When level with Pynes, take the gate in the corner of the field to enter a farmyard and immediately turn right through a small, way-marked, wooden gate to follow a wire fence on your right towards Pynes. Turn left in the corner to follow a wooden fence on your right around to a stile in it. Turn right over a stile to resume your former direction. A small, waymarked, wooden gate leads to a firm track through parkland. Go ahead to reach a road at a bend in it.

8. Bear left down the road to cross bridges over the railway and the River Credy. Go left along the pavement of the A377 back to the Cowley Bridge Inn.

2. Tipton St John

Route: Tipton St John – Hollow Head Cross – Wiggaton – Tipton St John

Distance: $5^1/_2$ miles

Map: O.S. Pathfinder 1315 Ottery St Mary

Start: The Golden Lion, Tipton St John (Grid Reference SY 091917)

Access: Tipton St John is served by bus no 382, which runs between Ottery St Mary and Sidmouth.

The Golden Lion (0404 812881)

Prince Philip supped here after floods devastated this area in 1968. You too can try real ale and be served with food. Bed and breakfast accommodation is available. The bar is open from 11 am to 3 pm and from 6 pm to 11 pm on weekdays, noon to 3 pm and 7 pm to 10.30 pm on Sundays.

Tipton St John

This quiet little village used to be a busy railway junction. A line branched off from the London and South Western Railway's main route between Salisbury and Exeter at Feniton. Opened in 1874, it ran south to Sidmouth. This was followed by a branch from Tipton St John to Budleigh Salterton in 1897 (extended to Exmouth in 1903). Sadly, both lines fell to Dr Beeching's axe in 1967.

The Walk

1. Go right to pass a telephone box on your right. Ignore the signposted public footpath on your left. Follow the road signposted for Ottery St Mary and Sidmouth. Climb to a crossroads and turn right for 150 yards, passing Tipton Cross bus stop.

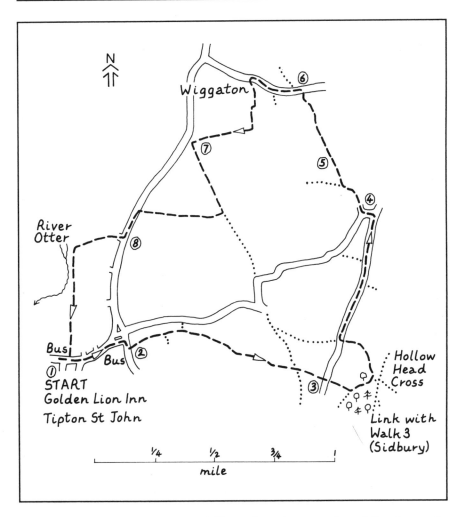

2. Turn left down steps to follow the signposted public footpath. Emerge over a stile in the corner of a field and go ahead beside a hedge on your left. Continue over a stile beside a gate in the next corner. Ignore the signposted path going right, then a signposted path going through a gate on your left to a road. Go ahead along the bridleway (waymarked with a blue arrow) and bear left at a fork to eventually reach a road.

3. Cross the road to take the signposted public footpath ahead and bear left to Hollow Head Cross (if you wish to link this route with Walk 3, go right at the top to a track).

4. Descend to the road, passing Badger's Rest. Turn right along the road. Ignore a signposted bridleway on your left but turn left at a road signposted for Tipton St John.

5. As the road bends left, turn right along a track, passing the newly-built Waxway Lodge on your left. Continue over a stile beside a gate and down a hedged track. Turn right through the first fieldgate and cross to a waymarked stile in the hedge opposite.

6. Bear very slightly left down to a stile in the hedge. Cross it and fork right down towards a stream. Continue over a stile and through a gate to follow a track down to a road.

7. Turn left along the road. Ignore a signposted public footpath on your right. Pass Cawley's Farm on your left. Ignore a track on your left soon after it. Reach 'Happy Valley' on your right and turn sharply left up a signposted public bridleway. This shaded old holloway bends right to reach a road.

8. Do not take the final steps to the road. Turn left along a hedged track. Approach a farm building and take an old green lane which runs between the hedges on your right to pass it on your left. Reach a junction and turn right to a road. Go left along it for 250 yards.

9. Turn right down the track to the old mill (this is a public footpath). A waymark post at the mill directs you through a gate ahead. Follow the waymarked path above the stream on your right all the way back to Tipton St John. This right of way has been cleared, waymarked and had stiles erected along it very recently, after being blocked for years. The mill-owners still dispute its existence but don't let them intimidate you. If you are told it is not a public footpath by the mill-owner (Mr Sargent), please write to Mr Linfoot, the Footpaths Secretary of the Devon Area of the Ramblers' Association, 14 Blaydon Cottages, Blackborough, Cullompton, Devon EX15 2HJ, who is taking a special interest in this path.

The Golden Lion, Tipton St John

3. Sidbury

Route: Sidbury – White Cross – Hollow Head Cross – Beacon Hill – Burscombe Farm – Sidbury

Distance: 5 miles

Map: O.S. Pathfinder 1315 Ottery St Mary

Access: Bus no 70 links Sidbury with Sidmouth and the nearest British Rail Station at Honiton

The Red Lion Inn (0395 597313)

Hot pennies used to be thrown out of the upstairs windows here at Sidbury Fair, held on the Wednesday before every 20th September. Food and real ale are available on any day, while you can also stay here on a bed and breakfast basis. The bar is open from 11 am to 2.30 pm and from 6 pm to 11 pm on weekdays, noon to 3 pm and 7 pm to 10.30 pm on Sundays.

Sidbury

This is an old settlement, with the hillfort on nearby Castle Hill dating from the New Stone Age. The Roman road from Dorchester to Exeter forded the River Sid at Sidford, just over one mile to the south. The hillfort was occupied as late as the 600s, perhaps until the invading Saxons won the decisive Battle of Penselwood over the Britons in 658. The church (dedicated to St Giles and St Peter) may have been a holy spot in British times, perhaps a very early Christian church. It boasts a Saxon crypt and 13th century wall paintings.

The East Devon Way

Buy some cider at Burscombe Farm!

Purple waymarks for this route, with a foxglove symbol, may be seen between Sidbury and White Cross. In case they whet your appetite to explore more of this new long distance trail, send an s.a.e. for current information on the East Devon Way to Geoffrey Jones, Rural Affairs Officer, East Devon District Council, Knowle, Sidmouth EX10 8HL. A guidebook should be available for this route which runs for some 40 miles between Exmouth and Uplyme.

The Walk

1. Go right and, opposite a telephone box on your left, bear right along the signposted public footpath to White Cross. Go ahead across a private road and along a hedged grassy track. Continue through two gates, the second of which has an East Devon Way waymark with a purple foxglove symbol. Go ahead beside a hedge on your right.

2. Go ahead over a waymarked stile in the corner, follow a hedge on your left to a stile beside a gate ahead. Bear right along a lane (soon ignoring a track which forks right). Pass Gorsemoor Farm on your right. Follow the track through a waymarked gate ahead.

3. Bear right through a waymarked gate at the end of the hedged track. Follow a hedge on your right to a waymarked gap in the top corner of this field. Cross the top of the next field and take the waymarked stile in the hedge facing you to follow lines of trees on your left to a stile in the next hedge. Continue over it, above trees on your left and across pasture to a stile and gate giving access to a track which leads to a road.

4. Turn right down the road for 40 yards to White Cross, then turn left along a woodland track (not the signposted public footpath which soon bears right from the track).

5. Reach Hollow Head Cross where you could bear right to link this route with Walk 2 from Tipton St John. Continue this route by taking the forest track ahead, as indicated by a purple arrow. Bear right at a fork and go through a gate to the Local Nature Reserve on Fire Beacon Hill.

6. Fork left through a sea of purple heather and yellow gorse. Turn left at a signpost and follow the broad path back to woodland. Go ahead to join a forest track at a public footpath signpost. Turn right along this track. Reach a Woodland Trust sign on your left, just before the track becomes a metalled lane and a field appears on your right.

7. Turn left along a woodland path. Climb to a ridge and descend to a corner formed by a field on your left. Cross a stile beside a gate to leave the wood and immediately turn right down pasture to a stile

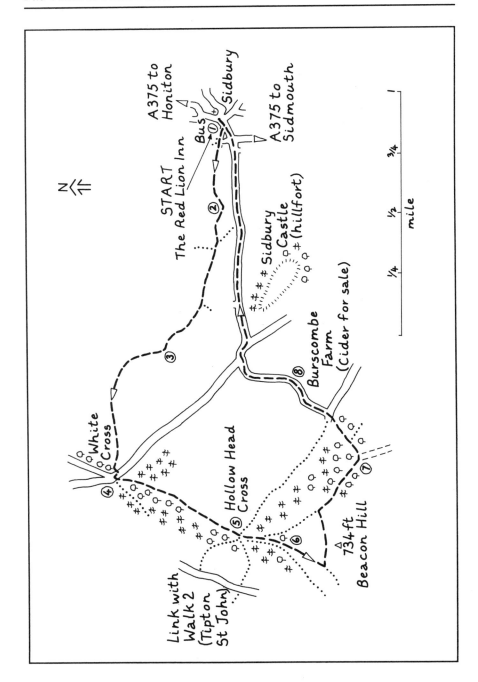

and steps giving access to a road junction. Take the descending road ahead of you to Burscombe Farm, where cider is made and sold (knock the door and ask to buy some).

8. Climb to a junction where you bear right and soon fork left to pass the wooded slopes of Sidbury Castle (hillfort) on your right. Go ahead to return to Sidbury and the Red Lion Inn.

4. Beer

Route: Beer – Beer Head – Hooken Cliffs – Beer

Distance: $2^1/_2$ miles

Map: O.S. Pathfinder 1316 Lyme Regis and Axminster

Start: The Barrel o'Beer (Grid Reference SY 229892)

Access: Bus no 378 serves Beer on its run between Sidmouth and Lyme Regis on Sundays and Bank Holiday Mondays during the summer season. This bus also connects with trains at Axminster station. During the week (Mondays to Saturdays except public holidays, throughout the year) there is the no 891 bus from Seaton, while the no 899 bus connects Sidmouth and Lyme Regis via Beer on weekdays.

The Anchor Inn (0297 20386)

Sir Winston Churchill supped here during the Second World War. Relax in the clifftop beer garden with real ale. Food and bed and breakfast accommodation are also available. The bar is open between 11 am and 11 pm on weekdays, noon and 3 pm, then 7 pm to 10.30 pm on Sundays.

The Barrel o'Beer (0297 20099)

This was made into a pub fairly recently after serving as a tollhouse in the 19th century. Real ale and food are served. Opening hours are 11.30 am to 11 pm on weekdays, noon to 3 pm and 7 pm to 10.30 pm on Sundays.

The Barrell o'Beer

Beer

How could a pub walks guide ignore a place named Beer? Actually, the word may come from the Saxon work 'bearu' meaning 'grove'. The Romans quarried stone here, so I expect that they (or, rather, their slaves) did have thirsts to quench. Beer stone can be seen used in Exeter cathedral. The notorious Jack Rattenbury was born in Beer in 1779. As an expert smuggler, he was called the Rob Roy of the West. It is easy to imagine him as you walk the authentic and picturesque streets down to the beach, littered with fishing boats. Children will love the model railway at Beer's Pecorama.

The Walk

1. Go right to reach the Anchor Inn and fork right up Common Lane. Approach the clifftop car park and fork left just before it to follow Little Lane.

2. Turn left, with the signposted Coast Path, before a caravan site. Take a kissing-gate and bear right beside a hedge. Keep above the sea on your left as you continue over two stiles.

3. Approach a third stile but turn right before it to follow the signposted public footpath to Hooken Cliffs. Walk with a fence on your left and go ahead over a stile to reach the Coast Guard lookout.

4. Turn sharply right along a signposted public footpath which soon merges with a rough track. Follow it over a cattlegrid in the corner and continue with a fence on your left.

5. Go ahead down a lane to pass the caravan site on your right as you return to Beer and its pubs.

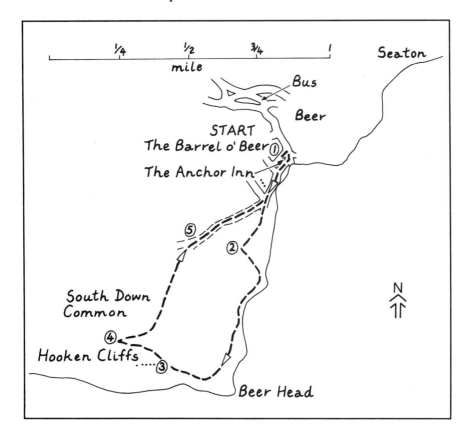

5. The Undercliff

Route: Axmouth – The Undercliff – Lyme Regis

Distance: 7 miles (one way)

Map: O.S. Pathfinder 1316 Lyme Regis and Axminster

Start: The Harbour Inn, Axmouth (Grid Reference SY 256911)

Access: This a a linear walk, so public transport comes into its own, with bus stops at each end. Bus no 899 links Axmouth and Lyme Regis on weekdays (except public holidays) throughout the year. This bus can also be used to reach Axmouth from Sidmouth. Bus no 378 provides a service from Sidmouth to Lyme Regis via Axminster railway station on Sundays and Bank Holiday Mondays during the summer. This doesn't call at Axmouth, but it does stop in Seaton, just two miles from Axmouth. If you are coming by car, park it in Lyme Regis and bus to the start of this walk so that you walk back to the car.

The Harbour Inn (0297 20371)

This is where the barmaid told me off for disturbing her! It seems a busy pub, however, serving real ale and food. The bar is open from 11 am to 2.30 pm and 6 pm to 11 pm on weekdays, noon to 2.30 pm and 7 pm to 10.30 pm on Sundays.

Axmouth

Hawkesdown Hill, immediately to the north of the village, is crowned by an ancient hillfort, haunted by a ghostly warrior. It guards the Icknield Way and the important track that became the Roman Foss Way. In the early years of the Roman conquests, this marked the frontier diagonally across Britain. It was breached in 49AD (six years after Claudius' invasion) when the Roman general (and future emperor) Vespasian captured Exeter, the capital of the Dumnonii. In those days the River Axe filled the estuary and large ships could safely find a harbour at Axmouth. The mouth of the river was gradually blocked by a shingle and pebble bank, behind which salt marshes formed. Even in the 16th century, John Leland found Axmouth a 'bigge Fischer towne', while Seaton was 'but a meane thing'. The Harbour Inn must be very old ('twas a pity about the bar maid). It stands opposite St Michael's Church. There was a church here in the second century, if not before. Beorn, King of the Angles, was murdered and buried here in 1049 (the body was later taken to Winchester). Medieval paintings have been uncovered inside the church. One vicar was William Hooke, a Puritan. His seditious sermons forced his departure to New England in 1639. He returned to Old England under the Commonwealth to become Oliver Cromwell's chaplain.

The Undercliff

This is an adventure! Enter on the understanding that there are no escape routes. Make for Lyme Regis or retrace your steps. Follow the route waymarked by the National Nature Reserve wardens and don't try to follow other paths with the aid of the map. Landslips cause changes while the woodland is jungle-like in its impenetrability. Not surprisingly, it is a rich habitat for wildlife, becoming an official reserve in 1955. There are 130 species of birds, many mammals (such as foxes, badgers, stoats and weasels), reptiles and amphibians, more than 30 species of butterflies, 200 species of moths, 400 different species of plants and so on. Bring a naturalist and you'd better bring a tent (except that camping is prohibited)! Geologists love the Undercliff too. They recognise three layers of rocks and soils here, causing one of the largest and best examples of land-slipping in the British Isles. Layers of chalk sit on top of greensand, letting water through to a clay base, which is waterproof and sloping slightly towards the sea. Rain causes the upper layers to become waterlogged, multiplying their weight. Wet clay also becomes slippery, so the heavier chalk and greensand slide down it towards the sea. A great landslip occurred at Christmas 1839. A chasm three quarters of a mile long, 300 foot wide and 150 foot deep formed when eight million tons of earth crashed in a single night.

Lyme Regis

This town is in Dorset and outside the scope of this book. However, if you wish to walk the Undercliff it makes sense to return to Axmouth by bus from here. The enormous stone Cobb shelters a sandy beach. West of the Cobb is the pebble beach where the Duke of Monmouth landed in 1685. He was welcomed and proclaimed king here. Thus began the unsuccessful Pitchfork Rebellion against the Roman Catholic James II. Jane Austen came here in 1803 and set part of her tender love story *Persuasion* in Lyme. She took lodgings near the Cobb. Look for the staircase known as 'Granny's Teeth' from which Louisa jumped into Captain Wentworth's arms in the novel.

The Harbour Inn, Axmouth

The Walk

1. Go left, passing St Michael's Church on your right. Fork right along Chapel Street. Pass Kemp's Lane on your left and Glenwater Close on your right. Fork right up Stepps Lane and pass a waymarked public footpath on your left.

2. Turn sharply right along a signposted public bridleway to link with the Coast Path. Turn left at the signposted junction to follow the Coast Path to Lyme Regis. Heed the notice stating that this is tough going through the almost

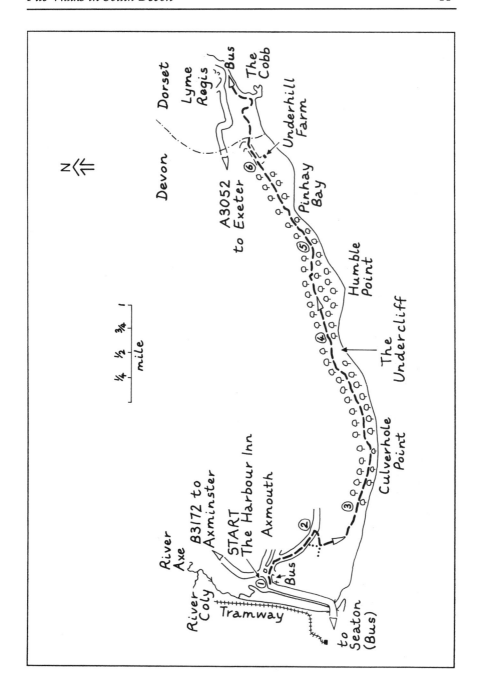

jungle-like woodland of the Undercliff. There are no escape routes, so allow plenty of time to complete the seven miles to Lyme Regis. Navigation is easy, with an obvious route improved by steps in places and yellow waymarking. Follow the waymarked path through the fields towards the sea.

3. Reach the National Nature Reserve information board and cross a stile to plunge into the Undercliff.

4. Reach a signpost and bear left for Lyme Regis (now four miles away). After 20 yards, fork right up the waymarked route, disregarding the line of the right of way as shown on the map.

5. Reach a signpost near a small water pumping station. Continue along the Coast Path towards Lyme Regis. This is a tarmac track for about half a mile then, as the lane climbs up to Pinhay, fork right with the waymarked Coast Path. Eventually emerge at another National Nature Reserve information board.

6. Take the lane ahead (ignoring a track to Underhill Farm on your right). Continue past a bungalow to reach a signpost. Bear right with the Coast Path through a kissing gate. Go ahead through a second kissing gate to enter Dorset. Bear right at a fork to enjoy a view over the sea on your right. Follow the signposted Coast Path as it bears right again, crosses a stream and follows a hedge on your right. Turn right over a stile to descend to The Cobb, Lyme Regis. Go left to pass this harbour and the beach on your right to reach The Square, Lyme Regis, where there is a bus stop for services to Axmouth (on Sundays and Bank Holidays you'll have to take the bus back to Seaton).

6. Exmouth

Route: Exmouth – Coast Path – Budleigh Salterton – Littleham – Exmouth

Distance: 11 miles

Map: O.S. Pathfinder 1330 Sidmouth

Start: The South Western (Grid Reference SY 001811)

Access: There is a good train service from Exeter, while Exmouth is also easy to reach by bus, including no X57, which runs between Exeter and Sidmouth via Exmouth and Budleigh Salterton.

The South Western (0395 263649)

This pub is full of railway memorabilia. Its name refers to the London and South Western Railway, who competed with the G.W.R. on routes

between London and Exeter. The L.S.W.R. opened its standard gauge line between Exeter and Exmouth in 1861. Bar opening hours are from 11 am to 11 pm on weekdays, noon to 3 pm and 7 pm to 10.30 pm on Sundays.

The Deer Leap
(0395 265030)

This pub overlooks the Exe estuary and serves real ale and food between 11 am and 11 pm on weekdays, noon to 3 pm and 7 pm to 10.30 pm on Sundays.

Beachcombers Bar
(0395 323323)

Coast Path walkers are very welcome at this Haven Holidays facility. Food is available and the opening hours are 11 am to 3 pm and 6 pm to 11 pm from Mondays to Fridays, 11 am to 11 pm on Saturdays and noon to 3 pm, then 7 pm to 10.30 pm on Sundays.

The King William IV, Budleigh Salterton
(0395 442075)

Real ale is served here from 11 am to 2.30 pm and 7 pm to 11 pm on weekdays, noon to 3 pm and 7 pm to 10.30 pm on Sundays.

Exmouth

Exmouth is the oldest resort in Devon. Its two miles of sandy beaches are still popular, while current attractions include the Wonderful World of Miniature, passed by this walk. This is the home of the world's largest '00' model railway. There are 7500 feet of track indoors plus 1800 feet outside. Open daily from Easter to 31st October, it is also open at weekends during the winter.

Budleigh Salterton

This unspoiled resort's name means 'Budda's forest clearing and salt-works', referring to saltpans which were once worked at the River Otter's mouth. When you pass the Octagon, notice the plaque which records that Sir John Everett Millais painted his famous picture *The Boyhood of Raleigh* whilst staying in this house in 1870. Sir Walter Raleigh was born a couple of miles inland at Hayes Barton, near East Budleigh. This route can be linked with Walk 7 to take you on a good day's walk of nearly 20 miles to the Sir Walter Raleigh Inn, East Budleigh.

Littleham

Visit the church of St Margaret and St Andrew. Francis (Fanny), Lady Nelson was buried here in 1831. Hers is the only tomb surrounded by iron railings.

The Walk

1. Take the pelican crossing and go left to bear right past the memorial garden on your left. Bear left up the Strand to pass the town hall on your right. Bear right at a roundabout. When a road called The Beacon forks left, take the signposted Plantation Walk just below it. Bear right at a fork to emerge beside The Deer Leap pub.

2. Cross the road and turn left along the promenade with the beach on your right. Pass the lifeboat, then the Wonderful Works of Miniature

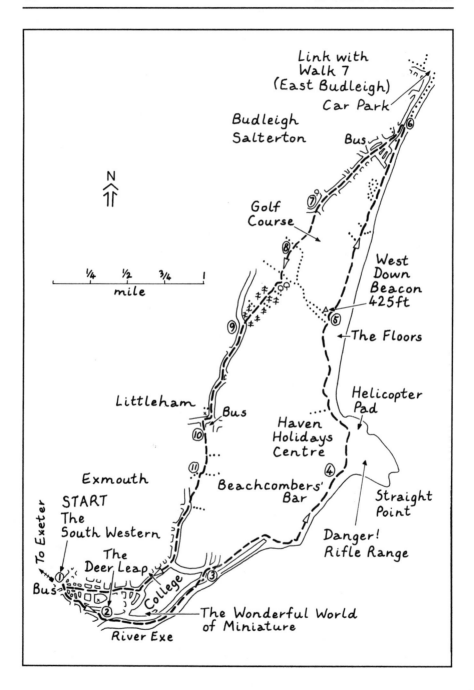

Link with
Walk 7
(East Budleigh)
Car Park

Budleigh
Salterton

Bus

⑥

N
⇑

Golf
Course

⑦

¼   ½   ¾   I
mile

⑧

West
Down
Beacon
425ft

⑤

←The Floors

⑨

Helicopter
Pad

Littleham   Bus

Haven
Holidays
Centre

⑩

Exmouth

⑪

Beachcombers'
Bar

④

Straight
Point

START
The
South Western

Danger!
Rifle Range

To Exeter

The
Deer Leap

①

College

③

Bus

②

The Wonderful World
of Miniature

River Exe

on your left. Bear left when the road forks and turn right at a crossroads to follow Foxholes Hill (a No Through Road) for the length of the carpark on your right.

3. Bear right along the signposted Coast Path to Sandy Bay and Budleigh Salterton. The metalled path rises well above the beach on your right. Continue across the National Trust's High Land of Orcombe and pass holiday chalets on your left to reach Beachcombers' Bar.

4. Follow the signposted Coast Path past the Royal Marines Ranges on your right. Continue past the helicopter pad and admire the magnificent red sandstone cliffs known as The Floors beyond that.

5. Follow the Coast Path over West Down Beacon (425 foot above sea level) and down to Budleigh Salterton.

6. Turn left along South Parade and enter Fore Street. The house immediately on your right is the Octagon (notice the plaque). Pass the Tourist Information Centre and the King William IV pub on your left. Continue up West Hill.

7. At the top of West Hill, pass Links Road on your left and, as the Exmouth Road bears right, go ahead along the signposted Littleham Church Path. Pass a golf course on your left, take a waymarked kissing-gate into the corner of a field ahead and follow a hedge on your right to a signpost.

8. Go ahead as signposted for Littleham. Cross open downland to a kissing-gate in the hedge ahead. Cross more of the golf course to reach a shady track. Bear left to follow the signposted Littleham Church Path. Skirt the golf course on your right, as waymarked by a yellow arrow, then take the path into woodland on your left. Soon, cross a waymarked stile and go ahead to a road (Castle Lane).

9. Turn left down the road to Littleham. Pass the Church of St Margaret and St Andrew and turn right up Littleham Road, then go left down Elm Lane. Pass a school on your right and take the hedged public footpath ahead to a metal kissing-gate.

10. Continue beside a hedge on your right. Cross a stile beside a gate in the next corner. Pass Green Farm on your right and go ahead through

another kissing-gate to walk with a stream on your left. After two more kissing-gates, bear slightly right away from the stream. Take a kissing-gate situated between two fieldgates in the hedge ahead. Follow the enclosed path to a junction.

11. Turn right and bear left with the hedged path, ignoring a stile on your right. Reach a road and go left down Douglas Avenue. Turn right along Rolle Road and go ahead at a roundabout back to the town centre and The South Western.

7. East Budleigh

Route: East Budleigh – Bicton Park – River Otter – Budleigh Salterton – East Budleigh

Distance: 7 miles

Map: O.S. Pathfinder 1330 Sidmouth

Start: The Sir Walter Raleigh Inn (Grid Reference SY 066849)

Access: East Budleigh is served by bus no X57 (Exeter – Exmouth – Budleigh Salterton – East Budleigh – Sidmouth)

The Sir Walter Raleigh (0395 442510)

This pub with the famous name does indeed date from the 16th century and must have been known to Raleigh. Real ale and food are available, as is bed and breakfast accommodation. Opening hours are 11.30 am to 3 pm and 6 pm to 11 pm on weekdays, noon to 3 pm and 7 pm to 10.30 pm on Sundays.

East Budleigh

Sir Walter Raleigh was born at Hayes Barton just over one mile west of the village. The family used to worship in the parish church and their pew is dated 1537. Bicton Park was laid out by Henry Rolle in the early 18th century. Its designer, Andre le Notre, did a similar job for the grounds of Versailles. One of the finest old gardens in England, it is open from March to October daily between 10 am and 6 pm. There are more than 60 acres of colour, fragrances and distinctive styles, including a classical Italianate garden. Trees abound, while blooms are tended in greenhouses. The Palm House contains a tropical rain-forest, while there is also a Countryside Museum and a Bicton Woodland Railway. The riverside dyke was built by Napoleonic prisoners of war.

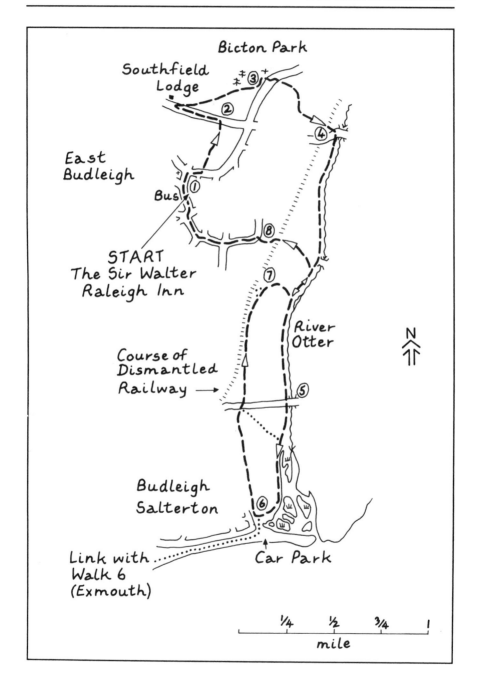

Bicton Park

Southfield
Lodge

East
Budleigh

Bus

START
The Sir Walter
Raleigh Inn

Course of
Dismantled
Railway →

River
Otter

N
⇑

Budleigh
Salterton

Link with
Walk 6
(Exmouth)

Car Park

¼   ½   ¾   1
mile

The Walk

1. Go right to pass the church (All Saints) on your left. Fork right up Vicarage Road and, after 200 yards, turn left up a signposted public footpath which goes through a kissing-gate. Continue with a hedge on your left past a sportsfield on your right. Bear right to cross a stile in the hedge ahead and walk with a hedge on your right to a stile giving access to a road.

2. Go left along the road and reach Southfield Lodge on your right. Turn sharply right along the signposted public bridleway, passing fields of pigs on your left. Descend to a gate and turn right through it to walk with a hedge on your left to a track. Bear right along this past woods on your left towards the A376 road.

3. Turn left to St Mary's Church, Bicton. Turn right with the walled path to reach the A376, cross this road carefully and go left for 30 yards, then bear right down a signposted public footpath. Follow a stream on your left and cross it by a small footbridge to put it on your right. Go ahead over the course of the dismantled railway (from Tipton St John to Exmouth) and reach a road.

4. Go left towards a bridge and turn right just before it to take the signposted public footpath to Budleigh Salterton. Walk with the River Otter on your left. Pass a footbridge on your left and ignore a track going right. Take a kissing-gate ahead to keep beside the river on your left.

5. Go ahead across a road and past a bridge on your left. Follow the signposted Coast Path towards Budleigh Salterton, passing through a nature reserve and above a cricket ground to reach a signpost. Let the Coast Path go left and go ahead to the next signpost.

6. Turn right along the signposted public footpath to White Bridge. Cross a lane to continue with the signposted public footpath. Follow the yellow arrows ahead as the track forks left.

7. Bear right to the River Otter and turn left to walk with it on your right. Bear left along a raised path. Cross the old railway again and reach a track.

8. Go left along a road which joins the A376 opposite the Rolle Arms. Cross the road carefully to pass the pub on your left as you continue into Lower Budleigh. Fork right up Middle Street to the High Street and the Sir Walter Raleigh.

The Sir Walter Raleigh

8. Dawlish

Route: Dawlish – Empson's Hill – Langstone Rock – Dawlish

Distance: 6 miles

Map: O.S. Pathfinder 1342 Newton Abbot

Start: The Marine Tavern (Grid Reference SX 963765)

Access: Take one of the most scenic stretches of railway line in the world to the station at Dawlish (on the main line between Exeter and Newton Abbot). Buses also link Dawlish with Exeter and Torquay (no 85) and Newton Abbot (no 85A)

The Marine Tavern (0625 865245)

Real ale, food and bed and breakfast accommodation are all available here. Bar opening hours are 11 am to 11 pm on weekdays, noon to 3 pm and 7 pm to 10.30 pm on Sundays.

Dawlish

Dawlish is derived from the Celtic for 'black stream' and compares with the Welsh Dulas. Dawlish Water flows from the old village through The Lawn of the genteel resort to the sea near the station on Brunel's Great Western Railway. The railway's arrival in 1846 made this a popular, if always sedate, resort. Jane Austen stayed in the old village in 1802, however. She loved the place and had Robert Ferrars remark to Elinor Dashwood in her novel *Sense and Sensibility* that it seemed rather surprising to him that anyone could live in Devon without living near Dawlish. Charles Dickens was fond of the place and placed the birth of his hero Nicholas Nickelby in a nearby farmhouse. Over 180 species of birds can be seen at Dawlish Warren in a year. This sandspit stretches for over one mile across the mouth of the Exe and includes a wildlife reserve with more than 450 different flowering plants. Relax on the beach after this walk.

Dawlish

The Walk

1. Cross the road and turn left, then turn right under the railway bridge. Go right along the seawall. Pass a footbridge over the railway on your right. Reach Coryton's Cove and turn right up steps and along a steep path. Fork left, up more steps. Pass another path on your right as you bear left to the viewpoint. Descend to the turning (now on your left) and take it this time to reach a road.

2. Go right, then pass Westcliff Road on your left but turn left immediately after it down Barton Lane, a narrow alley. Go ahead to its end, then turn right and right again at a T-junction. Almost immediately, bear left through the churchyard and pass the Church of St Gregory the Great on your right. Continue through a lych gate.

3. Turn left along a path which leads to a road junction. Go right, as signposted for Dawlish, cross a bridge and pass two turnings on your right before reaching Empsons Hill, the third. Turn right here and keep climbing until you reach a letterbox on your left, opposite a private road called 'The Humpty' on your right. Go ahead 40 yards to the next turning on your right.

4. Turn right along a track to a stile in the corner. Cross this to follow the hedge on your right to a gate in the next corner. Go through it and turn left (ignoring a stile on your right) for 30 yards. Turn right over a stile and walk with a hedge on your right to another stile at the summit of Empson's Hill, crowned by fir trees. Go ahead downhill beside a hedge on your left.

5. Continue over a stile to plunge down an enclosed path which emerges at a road. Go left, then turn right down Wallace Avenue. Keep descending to reach the main road and cross it to take a gap in the wall ahead and descend to a footbridge across the railway. Use it to reach the seawall.

6. What happens next depends on the state of the tide. If it is high, you cannot walk safely along the seawall, so take the Exeter road to direction no 7. If safe, turn left along the sea wall, with the railway on your left. Reach another railway bridge and turn left over it.

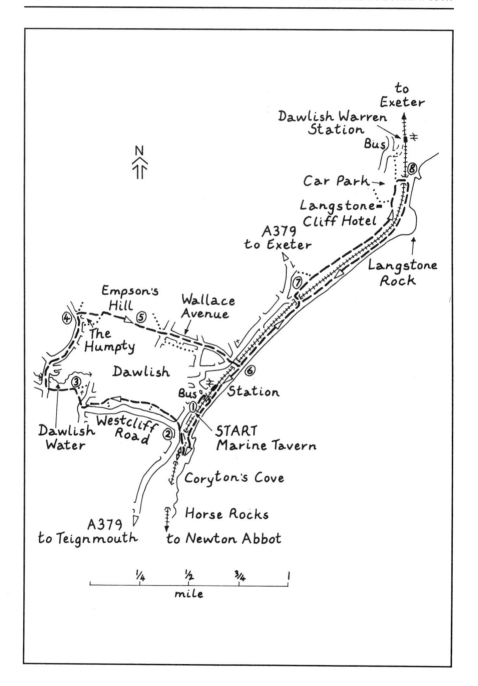

7. Turn sharply right along the clifftop path (the official Coast Path). Descend to pass Langstone Cliff Hotel on your left and reach a car park. Turn right over another railway footbridge.

8. Turn right to walk along the sea wall with the railway on your right. The beach may be an attractive alternative. Return under the railway bridge just after Dawlish station and go left back to the Marine Tavern.

9. Babbacombe

Route: 'Do It All' – Walls Hill – The Cary Arms – Babbacombe Model Village – Bygones

Distance: $2^1/_2$ miles

Map: O.S. Pathfinder 1351 Torquay

Start: Buses nos 32, 85 and 100 link the two ends of this walk. 'Do It All' is on Torquay's Babbacombe Road at Grid Reference SX 932649. Babbacombe Model Village is at Grid Reference SX 922658. It is possible to drive to the Cary Arms at Grid Reference SX 931654. Why not link this route with Walk 10 (Kent's Cavern)?

Access: Buses nos 32, 85 and 100 run up Babbacombe Road from Torquay's harbour. If you arrive in Torquay by train, it's an interesting and relaxing walk from the station with the sea on your right to the harbour.

The Cary Arms (0803 327110)

This old smuggler's den has a superb situation with fine views over Lyme Bay. Royalty have favoured the place with their presence on several occasions. The Prince of Wales came in 1829, Prince Albert called by in 1852 and the Prince of Wales (the future King Edward VII) brought his two sons, Albert and George, in 1880. Real ale and food are served, while self-catering accommodation is available. Opening hours are noon to 11 pm on weekdays, noon to 3 pm and 7 pm to 10.30 pm on Sundays.

John 'Babbacombe' Lee

There is one overwhelming reason to visit the Cary Arms and Babbacombe Beach. This secluded corner is the setting for a fascinating tale which has spawned films and songs in places as far apart as the U.S.A. and Australia. It concerns a murder and what happened to the 'murderer'. We will never be sure, but he was most probably John Lee. A

complex, moody, 20-year old, he was said to be descended from a family
of Dartmoor witches. He had a devoted girlfriend whom he told not to
see him anymore because he couldn't afford to marry her. She protested
in vain that love would overcome lack of money. He stole from his
employer, who allowed him a second chance and was known as a
'do-gooder'. He lived in her house opposite the Cary Arms, where the
public toilets now stand. His employer, Miss Keyse, also employed his
half-sister and she had a mysterious boyfriend who had made her
pregnant. On the night of 15th November 1884, Miss Keyse was murdered and an attempt was made to burn the evidence. Lee was arrested
and convicted of murder on circumstantial evidence. He maintained his
innocence to the last and told his gaolers on the morning of his execution
at Exeter Prison on 23rd February 1885, of a dream predicting that they
wouldn't be able to hang him. He was placed on the scaffold, the lever
was pulled but the trap refused to open. After three attempts, the
Authorities gave up and his sentence was commuted to life imprison-
ment. He was made to serve longer than usual, being released after 22
years in prison in 1907. He then cashed in on his fame, always maintain-
ing his innocence, married a woman in London, then abandoned her and
travelled around the world. Lee suggested that his half-sister's boyfriend
was the murderer but it is hard to believe it wasn't him – except for the
fact that he became 'the man they couldn't hang'.

Babbacombe

This is at the heart of the English Riviera, with fine beaches and many
other attractions. The Cliff Railway was originally built by the old
Torquay Tramways Company. Clustered near its top station are the
Babbacombe Model Village and Bygones. The Model Village is excep-
tionally interesting and the illuminations make a return visit at night
worthwhile. It is open every day except Christmas Day from 9 am to
dusk with evening illuminations extending the opening hours to 10 pm
from Easter to 30th September and 9 pm in October. Also open every
day except Christmas Day is Bygones, a Life Size Victorian Street, with
the inevitable model railway. 'Now with authentic smells', it is open
from 10 am to 10 pm from June to mid-September, to 5 pm from
mid-September to the end of October, from March to May and during
school holidays and every weekend, to 2 pm from November to February.

The Cary Arms

The Walk

1. Alight at the bus stop on Torquay's Babbacombe Road near the 'Do It All' DIY store. Facing 'Do It All', take the signposted public footpath to the right of the store. Follow it above 'Do It All' on your left. Emerge on downland at Walls Hill (a site of special scientific interest). Go ahead to join the clifftop.

2. Turn left to walk with the sea on your right. Divert right down steps to Redgate Beach. Climb back up to the clifftop and continue with the sea on your right.

3. Take the signposted Coast Path to Babbacombe. Go down steps to reach another signpost and go right along a lane for about 50 yards then bear right along the signposted Coast Path. Turn right at a waymark post before an arch. Descend and turn left as waymarked

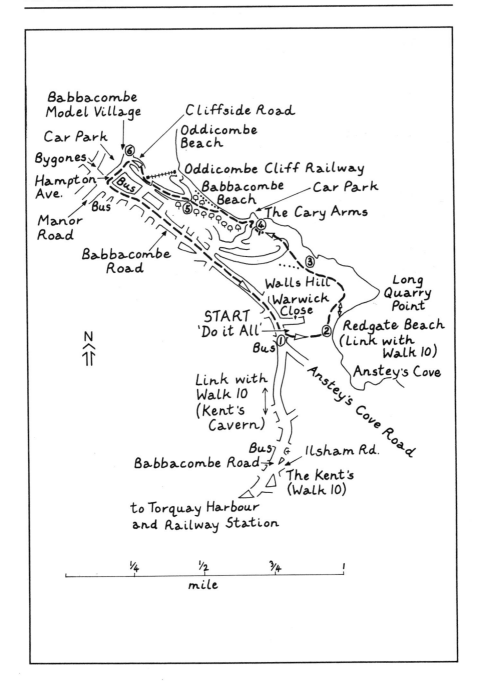

along an enclosed path and down steps to the Cary Arms, above
Babbacombe Beach.

4. Walk along the promenade above Babbacombe Beach on your right.
   Continue along a board walk around a cliff and up into woodland.
   Climb steps and keep ascending through the woodland to meet a
   road at a bend.

5. Bear left uphill to the top station of the Oddicombe Cliff Railway.
   Turn right along a path above this railway and continue up Cliffside
   Road. Cross the road at a junction and turn left. Babbacombe Model
   Village is immediately on your right.

6. Go ahead along Hampton Avenue. 'Bygones' is on your right at the
   end of this, at the corner with Fore Street. Turn left along Babbacombe Road. There is a bus stop to enable you to avoid walking
   along the pavement back down to 'Do It All', or to link with Walk 10
   at The Kent's, or to return to the harbour or railway station in
   Torquay.

10. Kent's Cavern

Route: The Kent's – Kent's Cavern – Thatcher Point – Hope's Nose – Anestey's Cove – The Kent's

Distance: 4 miles

Map: O.S. Pathfinder 1351 Torbay

Start: The Kent's, Torquay (Grid Reference SX 931641)

Access: Buses nos 32, 85 and 100 run up Torquay's Babbacombe Road to The Kent's from Torquay's harbour. If you arrive in Torquay by train, it's an interesting and relaxing walk from the station with the sea on your right to the harbour.

The Kent's (0803 292522)

Live jazz is an attraction here, along with the real ale and food. Opening hours are 11 am to 11 pm weekdays, noon to 3 pm and 7 pm to 10.30 pm on Sundays.

Kent's Cavern

The official guidebook is coy about the derivation of the name of this cave, but anyone familiar with *The Silbury Treasure* by Michael Dames would recognise the link with the Kennet or

Cunnit, the river whose 'swallowhead' is near Silbury, and with the Basque word *kuna*, meaning the female orifice. The Basques are the only living representatives of Neolithic European man. Amongst related English words is the obsolete 'cunicle', meaning a hole or passage underground. The ancient languages described the living earth and her parts as if she were the Great Mother, while women wise in such things as herbalism were described as 'cunning'. Prehistoric people have left abundant evidence of their acquaintance with this cave, with works of art, arrow-heads and knives formed out of flint. These date from at least 100,000 years ago. Evidence of later inhabitants include the skull of a young woman believed to be 20,000 years old. A visit is well worthwhile and the cave is open every day except Christmas Day, from 10 am to 9 pm in July and August (6 pm on Saturdays), to 6 pm in April, May, June, September and October, to 5 pm from November to March (closing at noon on Christmas Eve). The well-lit concrete paths are easy to walk and there is a constant temperature of 52°F, so bring warm clothing, even on a hot day.

Thatcher Rock

Tor(y) Bay is the spiritual home of the Conservative Party. It is well known that the spirits of Our Leaders set off into the great Blue beyond from a peninsula tipped by a firm, rocky, island. Well, here is the sacred spot resorted to by all Club members on a Monday. In honour of the Blessed Margaret, the ceremonial drive is named Thatcher Avenue. Some secret ritual must take place in Thatcher House before the assembled company traverse Thatcher Point to direct their task force to Thatcher Rock. As Torbay County Borough's Official Guide comments: 'the outcry when occasionally people land to explore the rocky surfaces must be heard to be believed'. If you are a redundant miner, take heart because just around the corner are Lead Stone and Ore Stone, off Hope's Nose. Yes, there is hope after Thatcher! The footpath above the delightful Anstey's Cove is called Bishop's Walk because Henry Phillpotts, a Bishop of Exeter had a seaside home here and loved this part of the Coast Path.

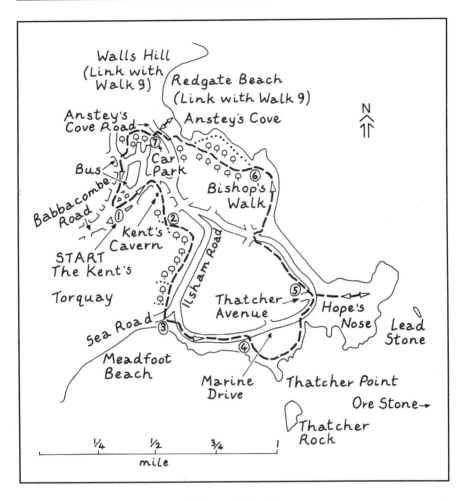

Walls Hill
(Link with
Walk 9)
Redgate Beach
(Link with Walk 9)
Anstey's
Cove Road
Anstey's Cove
N
Bus
Car
Park
Babbacombe
Road
Bishop's
Walk
Kent's
Cavern
START
The Kent's
Ilsham Road
Torquay
Thatcher
Avenue
Hope's
Nose
Lead
Stone
Sea Road
Meadfoot
Beach
Marine
Drive
Thatcher Point
Ore Stone
Thatcher
Rock

¼ ½ ¾
mile

The Walk

1. Go right, down Ilsham Road, as signposted for Kent's Cavern. Fork right as signed for Kent's Cavern Showcaves and take the public footpath past their entrance. Continue along a narrow path above a wooded slope. Fork right along a higher path.

2. Bear left, downhill, at the next path junction. Walk with woodland on your right and a park on your left then take a gap beside a metal

kissing-gate to bear left down towards Tor Bay. Cross the road to the car park for Meadfoot Beach.

3. Turn left with the signposted Coast Path to Ansty's Cove (2 miles). This climbs steps up a wooded cliff above the sea on your right to a top road. Turn right along its pavement.

4. Bear right down the signposted Coast Path to Thatcher Point. See Thatcher Rock on your right. Bear left back to the road which you turn right along. Pass Thatcher Avenue on your left to reach a signpost. A stile on your right gives access to Hope's Nose.

5. Back at the roadside signpost, go up steps beside it to follow the Coast Path above the road and the sea on your right. Descend to a roadside signpost and turn right to cross the road carefully and turn sharply right along the signposted public footpath for 'Bishop's Walk Anstey's Cove'. Turn left after 50 yards at the first signposted junction.

Looking north from Bishop's Walk

6. Fork left along the higher path and eventually reach a road opposite the car park for Anstey's Cove. Go right to a signposted path down to Anstey's Cove on your right. Back on the road, cross it to take a narrow path between the carpark and woodland.

7. Bear right up steps through the woodland. Emerge on the Babbacombe Road near a bus stop. Go left to return to The Kent's pub.

11. Bere Ferrers

Route: Bere Ferrers – Thorn Point – Liphill – Bere Ferrers

Distance: 4 miles

Map: O.S. Pathfinder 1349 Bere Alston

Start: The Olde Plough Inn (Grid Reference SX 460635)

Access: Come by train on the scenic line between Plymouth and Gunnislake

The Olde Plough Inn (0822 840358)

Sit in an attractive beer garden overlooking the Tavy estuary and sup real ale. Food is served, including vegetarian choices. This 16th century pub is full of atmosphere and includes gravestones in the bar (recycled from another site – this was never a graveyard). There is a ghost of a Victorian lady, probably a former landlady, who has been seen by some customers.

Bere Ferrers

Bere is said to be derived from 'birlanda', the Saxon for 'point of land', while Ferrers comes from the name of the Norman family who acquired this territory after the Battle of Hastings. They took their name from Ferriere, a village in Normandy. This area used to be famous for its cherry trees, while apples, pears, strawberries, plums and daffodils were also grown. The London and South Western Railway built its main line through Bere Alston and used it to rush the produce to London. That line no longer exists, but the surviving Tamar Valley Line between Plymouth and Gunnislake via Bere Ferrers and Bere Alston is a real joy to ride. A walk from another of its stations, on the Cornish side of the border at Calstock, features in *Pub Walks in Cornwall* by the same author and publisher as this book.

Take the train from Plymouth to Bere Ferrers

The Walk

1. Go left, uphill. Pass the well made by Frances Lady Shelley for the benefit of the poor in her son's parish in 1852. Reach a junction and turn left up the road signposted for the railway station as well as Clamoak and Holes Hole.

2. Do not turn right towards the station. Go straight ahead at this junction to follow a lane past bungalows on your right and a farm on your left. Continue under the railway bridge and turn left at the top.

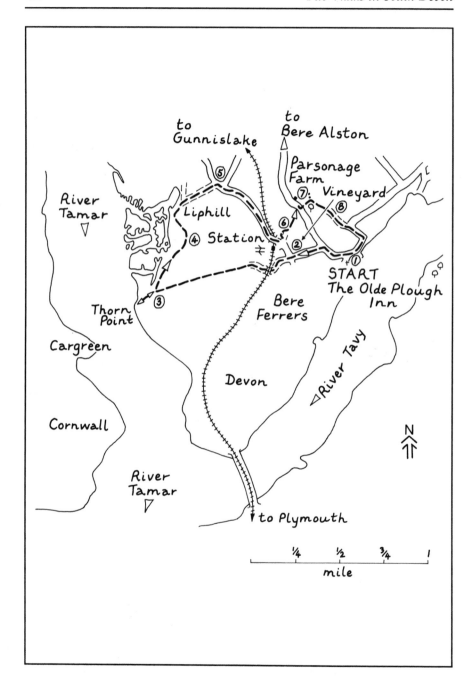

Cross a stile and follow a track through a field. Maintain your direction towards the Tamar estuary.

3. Your path will be to the right at the foot of the hill, but first divert over a stile to bear left to Thorn Point, where ferries used to land fresh strawberries and flowers from Cornwall. Retrace your steps back over the stile and turn left. Continue above the mudflats and saltmarshes on your left, over another stile and bearing right to pass between buildings.

4. Descend to the bottom left-hand corner of the field to take a gate and walk with Liphill Creek on your left. Bear right up the access drive of a house.

5. Turn right along a lane and continue over a bridge across the railway. Pass the station on your right and turn sharply left down a drive which has signs for Birlanda Vineyard, Tavy Court and the Coach House. Soon bear left, as signed for the Coach House. Approach the house but go to the left of the vegetable patch to reach a waymarked stile in the hedge.

6. Cross the stile and follow the enclosed path with a view of the Tavy estuary ahead for 20 yards, then turn left down the field towards Parsonage Farm. Cross the stile beside a gate and a signpost to reach a road.

7. Go right along the road for 40 yards then turn left over a wooden stepstile beside a signpost. Go uphill to pass a prominent beech tree and take a small, waymarked, metal gate in the top right-hand corner. Turn right through it and follow the narrow, enclosed, path. Continue over a waymarked stile, bear left then right to walk with a hedge on your right. Descend to a rough lane.

8. Go left down the rough lane to join a metalled road. Go right along this to pass a Methodist chapel on your right and the Tavy estuary on your left. Follow the road as it bears right to pass the Post Office on your left and reach the Olde Plough Inn soon after it.

12. Plym Valley Railway

Route: Marsh Mills – Plym Bridge – Riverford Viaduct – Woolwell

Distance: 5 miles (one way)

Maps: O.S. Pathfinder 1356 Plymouth and O.S. Outdoor Leisure 28 Dartmoor

Access: This is a linear walk on the outskirts of Plymouth, so take bus no 21 or 51 from Plymouth's Royal Parade to Marsh Mills, for the Plym Valley Railway. Walk to The George for buses nos 83, 84 and 84A back to the centre of Plymouth

The George (0752 771527)

Sunday evening here is Country and Western, while Friday is the Wheel of Fortune and Trivia Quiz. Real ale and food are served everyday in this old coaching inn. Bar opening hours are 11.30 am to 3 pm and 5.30 pm to 11.30 pm from Mondays to Thursdays, 11.30 am to 11 pm on Fridays and Saturdays, noon to 3 pm and 7 pm to 10.30 pm on Sundays.

The Plym Valley Railway

The South Devon and Tavistock Railway opened their line between Marsh Mills and Tavistock in 1859, extending to Launceston in 1865. It was a broad gauge (7ft $0^1/_4$ins) line, as was Brunel's Great Western main line, but it had a third rail added in 1876 to accommodate standard gauge (4ft $8^1/_2$ins) express trains run by the London and South Western Railway from Waterloo to Plymouth. This arrangement ceased when the L.S.W.R. took a new route via Bere Alston in 1890. Bank holidays before 1939 would see up to 20,000 passengers taking a trip on this line for a walk in the woods. Traffic declined severely in the 1950s and closure came on 29th December 1962, when bad weather left trains stranded at Bickleigh and Tavistock for two days. The track was lifted in 1964. Then the Plym Valley Railway was formed in 1980. It has plans to run trains

the Plym Valley Railway was formed in 1980. It has plans to run trains again from Marsh Mills to Plym Bridge. This section of the walk follows the Lee Moor Tramway, rather than the railway.

The George

The Walk

1. Walk away from Marsh Mills roundabout and turn left after the Comet superstore to pass a car park on your left. Come to the Royal Marines base ahead on your left and the headquarters of the Plym Valley Railway ahead on your right. Take the path between them.

2. Cross the road at Plym Bridge and go ahead over a stile to follow a path which runs above the river on your left. When level with a quarry across the river, fork right up a steep, wooded slope. Don't take a bridge ahead but do fork right to the cycleway.

3. Turn left along the cycleway to cross Cann Viaduct (you are now on

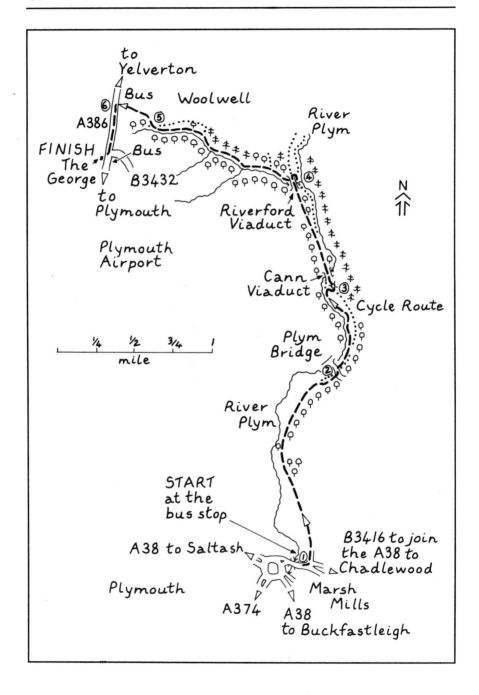

the old railway route). Continue to cross the Riverford Viaduct.

4. Turn right down the wooded slope to join the valley path and go right to a signpost under an arch of the Riverford Viaduct. Take the signposted footpath ahead to Woolwell ($1^1/_4$ miles), walking upstream with the stream on your left. Keep to this firm track, ignoring turnings to right and left.

5. A path converges on yours from the sharp right. Go ahead to bear right up a concrete track and reach the A386 (Tavistock Road).

6. Turn left along the pavement of the A386 to traffic lights at its junction with Plymbridge Road (B3432). This is at the corner of Plymouth City Airport. Turn right here to cross the road to The George.

13. Totnes

Route: Totnes – Windmill Down – Copland Meadow – Totnes

Distance: 4 miles

Map: O.S. Pathfinder 1341 Buckfastleigh and O.S. Outdoor Leisure 20 South Devon

Start: King William IV Inn (Grid Reference SX 804604)

Access: Totnes is on the mainline between Newton Abbot and Plymouth, so come by train. There are also buses from a variety of places, including the X80 (from Plymouth and Torquay), the 89 (from Dartmouth and Newton Abbot) and the 164 (from Kingsbridge). You could also reach Totnes by steam train from Buckfastleigh or take a boat trip from Dartmouth. This scenic river cruise features in the 'Round Robin' ticket along with buses between Totnes and Paignton and steam trains from Paignton to Kingswear. This ticket also covers the ferry from Kingswear to Dartmouth. You can start your journey at Totnes, Paignton, Kingswear or Dartmouth and break your journey at any time. The 1993 ticket price was £9.00 for an adult, £6.00 for a child, £8.00 for a senior citizen and £26.00 for a family.

King William IV Inn (0803 866689)

Built in 1830, this pub is convenient for the Brutus Stone. Bed and breakfast accommodation is available, while real ale and food are served. Opening hours are 11 am to 11 pm on weekdays, noon to 3 pm and 7 pm to 10.30 pm on Sundays.

The Castle Inn (0803 863274)

There is a ghost in the cellar of this inn, which was the West Gate Tavern in the Middle Ages. Real ale, food and bed and breakfast accommodation are all available. Opening hours are 11 am to 11 pm on weekdays, noon to 3 pm and 7 pm to 10.30 pm on Sundays.

The Bull Inn (0803 862042)

Keith Floyd, the television cook, likes to sup here. Real ale, food and bed and breakfast accommodation are available. Opening hours are 11 am to 11 pm on weekdays, noon to 3 pm and 7 pm to 10.30 pm on Sundays.

Totnes

Legend comes to life in Totnes for here is the very stone on which Brutus stepped ashore after his voyage from Troy and exclaimed:

'Here I sit and here I rest,
And this town shall be called Totnes'.

The stone happens to be up a hill from the river, but don't let that fact spoil a good story. Here is where Britain began the transition from

Albion. Of course, Brutus could have exercised his legs a little before sitting down on the stone. Brutus was the great grandson of Aeneas of Troy and the founder of the British race. Flint tools have been found here, as have Roman tiles, so the place is not without history. Totnes has much more character. The museum is housed in an Elizabethan Merchant's House in Fore Street. There is a special display on the work of Charles Babbage, the Totnes mathematician who was the 'father' of the computer. It is open from Mondays to Fridays between April and October (10.30 am to 1 pm and 2 pm to 5 pm).

East Gate, Totnes

The Normans built a castle on a hill overlooking the town in their characteristic motte-and-bailey style. A stone shell keep and curtain wall were built in the 13th century. It is now in the care of English Heritage and open between 10 am and 6 pm (closed for lunch between 1 pm and 2 pm) daily from April to September, then open between 10 am and 4 pm (closed for lunch between 1 pm and 2 pm) from Tuesdays to Sundays during the winter (closed at Christmas and New Year).

The Walk

1. Go right, up Fore Street. Pass the Brutus Stone on your right. Continue through the arch of the East Gate into High Street. Pass St Mary's Church on your right, then the Castle Inn (on the corner of Castle Street). Follow the road as it bears left but keep straight on when most traffic turns right. Pass The Bull inn on your left and reach the A381. Cross this road carefully.

2. Go ahead up the rough lane signed as being 'Unsuitable for Motors'. Continue to a road and turn right along it for about half a mile.

3. Bear right down a track and go right when it forks. Reach a crossroads and take the road ahead, as signposted for Dartington. Continue over a railway bridge.

4. Turn right along an old green lane. Emerge to an estate road, Copland Meadow. Bear right to a road junction at Barracks Hill.

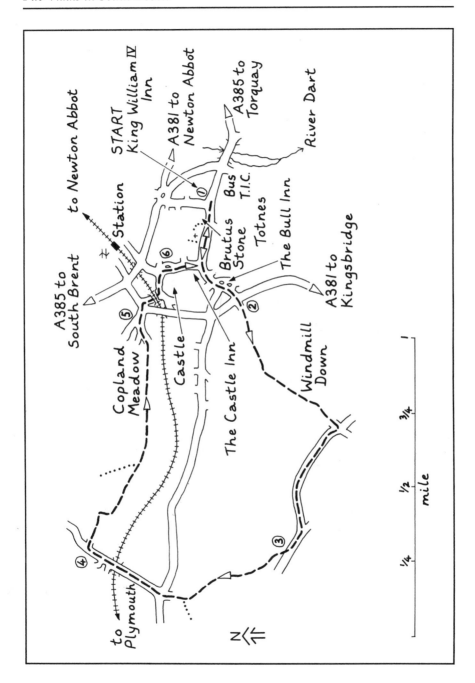

5. Go right to a T-junction, cross the main road carefully and bear left, then turn right almost immediately at Malt Mill. Continue under a railway bridge, cross the road and bear left. Turn right into Castle Street.

6. Take a narrow path ahead and continue to Totnes Castle, on your right. Maintain your direction along Castle Street and turn left when it joins High Street. Go through the East Gate to return down Fore Street to the King William IV pub.

14. Plymouth Hoe

Route: The Minerva – Plymouth Gin Distillery – Mayflower Steps – Plymouth Hoe – St Andrew's Church – The Minerva

Distance: 2 miles

Map: O.S. Pathfinder 1356 Plymouth

Start: The Minerva, Looe Street, Plymouth (SX 482544)

Access: The Minerva is near Plymouth's Bus Station. Trains come to Plymouth from all over the country. The railway station is a 15-minute walk down Armada Way and along Royal Parade to the bus station.

The Minerva (0752 669065)

Sir Francis Drake drank here and was playing bowls at the back of this pub (and not on the Hoe) when the Armada was sighted. Dating from the 15th century, one late 16th century addition was a spiral staircase built around the mast from a Spanish galleon. The oldest pub in Plymouth, it can boast a ghost in Tudor dress (seen recently by the landlord's son). Real ale is served with a smile and the opening hours are noon to 3 pm and 7 pm to 11 pm from Mondays to Fridays, noon to 11 pm on Saturdays, 7 pm to 10.30 pm (evenings only) on Sundays.

Plymouth

Plymouth is a city that will live long in the memory. This walk takes you to the old harbour and the famous Hoe, but set time aside for a boat trip and to visit the shopping centre. The view over the Sound is the most memorable thing, however. Shut your eyes and imagine Drake sailing out to fight the Spanish Armada. *The Mayflower*, too, set sail from here. Sailing in came the ingredients for Plymouth Gin, whose distillery is visited by this walk. Smeaton's Tower stands on the Hoe now. Built in 1759 on the treacherous Eddystone Rocks, it was removed to here when a larger lighthouse replaced it in 1882. Below it is the modern Plymouth

Smeaton's Tower

Dome which brings the history of Plymouth to life with its displays. This is open daily (except Christmas Day) from 9 am (open till late on summer evenings). Nearby is the Aquarium of the Marine Biological Association. King Charles II built the Citadel after the townspeople had declared for Parliament in the Civil War. The citadel is built over the site of the figure of a giant that was cut in the grass. Periodic scouring of it was recorded, as in 1541 when William Hawkyne was paid 8d for doing the job. The giant was then described as Gogmagog, the last of the giants of Albion. The rest were exterminated when Brutus arrived in Totnes to change the island's name to Britain and to populate it with Trojans (according to Geoffrey of Monmouth in the early 12th century). One Trojan was partial to giants. He was Corineus, so he was given this part of the country to rule and deal with Gogmagog. Corineus wrestled with Gogmagog on the Hoe and threw him to his death on the rocks below. Whatever the substance of this legend, the carved figure of the giant was real until the reign of Charles II. The Trojan link was probably invented, but Gogmagog, whose gigantic bones and teeth were uncovered when the foundations of the Citadel were being dug, could have been Ogmios (identified as Hercules).

Miraculously, the Elizabethan lanes of the Barbican escaped destruction in World War II. Margaret of Anjou landed here in 1470 to meet her future husband, Henry VI. Catharine of Aragon came ashore here, while Captain Cook set sail from here for Australia. The Tolpuddle Martyrs were to follow from the same place. Few places have seen such distinguished coming and going.

Hitler's bombs did destroy Plymouth's mother church, dedicated to St Andrew, the patron saint of fishermen. Only the walls were left standing but a cross was soon formed, out of burnt wood and appeared with the word 'Resurgam' (I will rise again) above the scarred door. Visit the rebuilt church and, close by, Prysten House. Built in 1490, this started life as a lodging house for priests, then became a smugglers' den before being bought by a wine merchant. The restored Merchant's House, nearby, is a museum of Plymouth's social and economic history.

The Walk

1. Go right down Looe Street and turn right along Vauxhall Street to reach the harbour area of the Barbican on your left. Bear left to pass The Three Crowns on your right and go up the cobbled Parade to see Robert Lenkiewicz's mural beside his studio. Take the passageway to the left of these, called Blackfriar's Ope, to reach Southside Street and, facing you, the Plymouth Gin Distillery.

2. Facing the distillery, go left along Southside Street. Pass the old fish market on your left then Island House (where the Puritans were entertained before departing on the Mayflower) on your right. American and British flags on your left mark the Mayflower Steps.

3. Go ahead with the harbour on your left (with boat trips from Phoenix Wharf) towards the Hoe and sea front. Follow Madeira Road past the Sound on your left, below the Citadel on your right. Cross Hoe Road to walk on the Hoe to Smeaton's Tower. The Plymouth Dome is below.

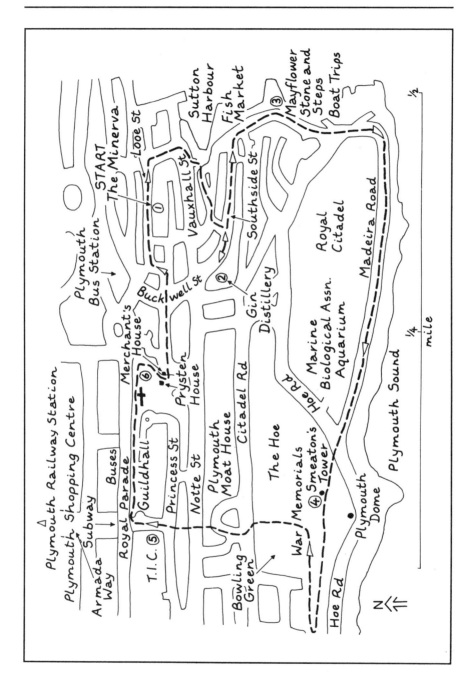

4. Continue along the Hoe above Plymouth Sound on your left. At the end of the grass, retrace your steps to the war memorials and turn left, inland. Pass a bowling green on your left and Plymouth Moat House (a hotel) on your right. Take the pelican crossing over Notte Street to pass fountains and cross Princess Street to reach the Tourist Information Centre on your left.

5. Go right to pass the Royal Parade subway, with its outstanding murals, on your left. Pass the Guildhall on your right, then St Andrew's Church.

6. Turn right down St Andrew Street and bear right to Prysten House. Go down to the Merchant's House, on your left and turn left to pass it and take Palace Street to Buckwell Street. Go ahead over it then turn left up Peacock Lane to emerge at the top of Looe Street. Turn right down Looe Street to return to the Minerva.

15. Bovisand Bay

Route: Hooe – Turnchapel – Bovisand Bay – Hooe

Distance: $5^1/_2$ miles

Map: O.S. Pathfinder 1356 Plymouth

Start: The Victoria Inn (Grid Reference SX 499525)

Access: Take the no 7 bus from Plymouth's Royal Parade to Hooe Lake

---

The Victoria Inn, Hooe (0752 405196)

This 'village' pub is full of character and characters. Darts is an extremely popular game, while real ale and snacks are served. Opening hours are 11 am to 2.30 pm and 6.30 pm to 11 pm from Mondays to Fridays, 11 am to 11 pm on Saturdays, noon to 3 pm and 7 pm to 10.30 pm on Sundays.

The Victoria

The Royal Oak

The Royal Oak Inn, Hooe (0752 403822)

This pub is a treasure chest, full of artefacts, including a bottle collection. Dating from the 17th century, it provides bed and breakfast accommodation as well as real ale and food. Vegetarians are catered for. Opening hours are 11 am to 3 pm and 7 pm to 11 pm on weekdays, noon to 3 pm and 7 pm to 10.30 pm on Sundays.

The Boringdon Arms, Turnchapel (0752 402053)

'Plymouth Pub of the Year' in 1993, this building dates from the 1730s when it was the quarrymaster's house in the Saltram Estate (the quarry provided limestone for the kilns passed on this walk). Given by the crown to the Parker family, one son acquired the title and arms of Lord Borington (his brother became Lord Morley and shared the same coat of arms). Real ale, food and bed and breakfast accommodation are all available. Opening hours are 11 am to 11 pm on weekdays, noon to 3 pm and 7 pm to 10.30 pm on Sundays.

Jennycliff

The Coast Path begins by taking you over Jennycliff, with its marvellous views of Plymouth, Drake's Island and Cornwall. One small ridge of this coastline is known as 'Abraham's Garden' because Spanish slaves were buried on it during the plague of 1665.

Mount Batten Point has been a strategic spot for thousands of years and is one candidate for the Ictis of the ancient tin trade (see also *Pub Walks on the Isle of Wight* by the same author and publisher as this book for more on Ictis). Once known as Haw Stert, it acquired its modern name when Admiral Batten defended it during the siege of Plymouth in the Civil War. T.E. Lawrence (Lawrence of Arabia) served on Flying-boats here under the name of Aircraftsman Shaw from 1920 to 1935.

Fort Stamford was part of Palmerston's defensive measures against possible French attack. Started in 1845, it was completed in 1847 at a cost of £13,787 12s 7d. The Fort at the centre of the Breakwater dates from this time too. The Breakwater's foundation stone was laid by the Prince Regent in 1812 but the last of its four million tons of stone wasn't in place until 1842. It is over one mile long.

The Walk

1. Go right and turn right along Lake Road to the Royal Oak. Facing this pub, go left to walk past a playground on your left and with the bay of Hooe Lake on your right. Follow a lane around the bay and pass 18th century lime kilns on your left. Continue past the Royal Marines base on your right (539 Assault Squadron) and the Boringdon Arms on your left.

2. Fork left to pass above the New Inn on your right. Follow the road around a corner on your left where, until it was stolen in 1993, a plaque recorded the fact that T.E. Lawrence (Lawrence of Arabia, 1888-1935) was stationed here in the flying boat squadron from 1929 to 1935. He was then known as Shaw. Turn right at the top junction to pass Fort Stamford Leisure Centre on your left.

3. When the road bends left, take a gap ahead to follow the Coast Path beside a fence on your left and with a view over Plymouth Hoe on your right. Climb a grassy slope to a road and go right along it.

4. Bear right down the signposted Coast Path to Bovisand Bay until Plymouth Breakwater and Bovisand Pier are on your right. Ignore steps going up on your left.

5. Go left along a lane, keeping above the bay on your right. Fork right at a hairpin bend and bear right along the signposted Coast Path down to the beach.

6. Turn left inland along a waymarked path which runs beside a fence on your right and up a valley to converge with a lane. Continue as signposted for Staddiscombe, following a rough track while the lane turns right into Bovisland Lodge Estate. Go straight ahead along a delightful old green lane to emerge through a gate to the corner of a metalled lane. Turn left along it to a junction.

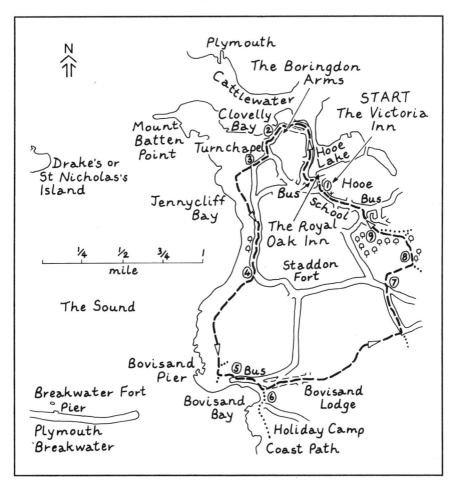

7. Turn left along the road for 10 yards, then bear right across the road
   to take a kissing-gate and go ahead along a well-trodden fieldpath.
   Continue through a kissing-gate in the next fence and turn right to
   follow a fence which becomes a hedge on your right. Approach
   woodland and turn left to pass this on your right.

8. Go ahead into the next field where the hedge is now on your left.
   Continue through a gap in the corner of more woodland to follow a
   path straight ahead down its left-hand edge. At the next corner
   descend 20 yards and fork left. Keep left at a lower fork and descend
   to a firmer path.

9. Bear left to pass a housing estate on your right and take a No
   Through Road (Arscott Lane). Fork right along Belle Vue Road to
   Hooe Road and go left to reach the Victoria Inn (on your right).

16. Yealmpton

Route: Yealmpton – Kitley Caves – The Shire Horse Centre – Higher Torr – Yealmpton

Distance: 4 miles

Map: O.S. Pathfinder 1356 Plymouth

Start: The Volunteer (Grid Reference SX 578518)

Access: Yealmpton can be reached by bus no 93 (Plymouth – Dartmouth) and bus no 94 (Plymouth – Noss Mayo)

The Volunteer (0752 880462)

Called 'The Rifle Volunteer' in the early 19th century, this is where many Queen's Shillings were spent. The lounge is haunted by a black shadow, usually seen by females. It is not to be confused with 'Giant' Haystacks, a wrestler, who once stayed here. Ian Botham has also passed through on a long distance walk. Real ale and food (including vegetarian) are served. Opening hours are 11 am to 11 pm on weekdays, noon to 3 pm and 7 pm to 10.30 pm on Sundays.

Yealmpton

Sir John Betjeman found St Bartholomew's to be 'the most amazing' church. A monument inscribed with the name Toreus links the site with the Roman period. This stone pillar stands in the churchyard. Inside the church is a Saxon font.

Kitley is where Sarah Martin composed the rhyme about Old Mother Hubbard in 1805. Kitley Caves contain flint tools made by prehistoric men but remained undiscovered for thousands of years until the local limestone quarrymen accidentally uncovered a cave entrance in the early 1800s. The caves are beautiful and dramatic, while research is ongoing.

A visit is recommended. Kitley Caves are open daily from Good Friday until the end of October between 10 am and 5.30 pm.

The National Shire Horse Centre

The Shire Horse Centre is open throughout the year (except from 24th to 26th December) between 10 am and 5 pm (4 pm in winter). There are lots of events in the summer, such as the Steam and Vintage Rally on the second weekend in August.

The Walk

1. Cross the road to the bus stop for Plymouth and turn right along the pavement for 30 yards then turn left down steps. Follow an enclosed path and turn right along a lane, passing St Bartholomew's Church on your right. Continue along a grassy path past a playground on your right.

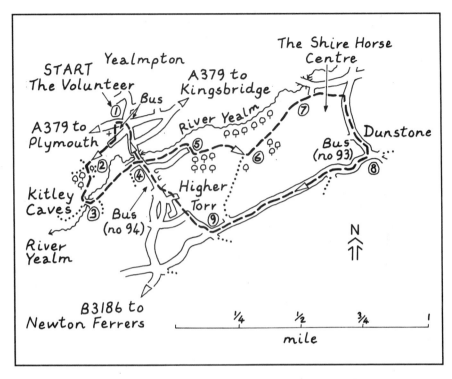

2. Do not take the track going left at the end of the field to a waterworks. Go ahead to a track junction and turn left through woodland to reach a footbridge on your left (ignore a preceding rope bridge). Visit Kitley Caves, on your right, before turning left across the footbridge.

3. Ignore the adventure playground on your left and take a broad track through woodland. Pass a path going right where the old railway once had a bridge. Go ahead above the River Yealm on your left. Emerge along a lane and pass houses on your right (Boldventure leading to Waltacre).

4. Cross the road to pass a bridge on your left and take the waymarked path through the small gate ahead. Follow a narrow path above the river on your left, then bear right to a stile and go right to another stile at the end of an estate road.

5. Cross the stile and immediately bear left past a house named 'Sidings' and up a signposted public footpath to woodland. Turn left along the edge of the wood, on your right. Continue over a stile and across a field with a hedge on your left. Take a stile into the next field and bear right diagonally up it to a stile in its far corner. Cross the stile.

6. Follow a hedge on your right to a stile in the next corner and maintain this direction (n.b. a popular unofficial route is through the fields to the left of what may be an overgrown path).

7. Go ahead over a stile in the corner formed by hedges jutting out in front of you. Pass a sign beside this stile stating 'Any person found straying from the Public Footpath will be prosecuted. By Order – The National Shire Horse Centre Ltd'. The Shire Horse Centre is away to your right, so keep well clear of it! Follow the enclosed path ahead, cross a lane and continue along a signposted path. Reach a road and turn right to pass the entrance to the Shire Horse Centre on your right. Continue to Dunstone.

8. Turn right along the lane signposted for Torr.

9. Turn right, as signposted for Yealmpton. When the lane bends left, go ahead along a signposted path running beside a brook on your left. Continue over an estate road and follow the path to the B3186. Turn right to pass Ploughman Way on your right and cross the road to Torre Cottage to continue along the pavement. Go ahead over the footbridge to the left of the road bridge. Climb Torr Hill (signposted for Plymouth and Brixton). Reach Market Street and go left to The Volunteer.

17. Ermington

Route: Ermington – Sequer's Bridge – Ermington

Distance: $2^1/_2$ miles

Map: O.S. Pathfinder 1357 Ivybridge

Start: The Crooked Spire Inn (Grid Reference SX 637531)

Access: Bus no 91 runs through Ermington on its way between Dartmouth and Plymouth on Mondays, Wednesdays and Fridays. There are also buses nos 608 (from Ivybridge on Thursdays), 612 (Yealmpton – Ivybridge on Tuesdays) and 614 (Plympton – Totnes on Fridays). You may well prefer to start at Sequer's Bridge because the frequent daily service no 93 (Plymouth – Dartmouth) stops nearby.

The Crooked Spire Inn (0548 830202)

You need only look to the church up the road for the inspiration behind this pub's name. Dating from the 17th century, it serves real ale and food as well as offering bed and breakfast accommodation. Opening hours are 11.30 am to 2.30 pm and 6.30 pm to 11 pm on weekdays, noon to 3 pm and 7 pm to 10.30 pm on Sundays.

Ermington

The 'best kept village in South Hams' in 1985 and 1986 acquired its distinctive church spire when it bowed to a beautiful bride as she came to be married at the church. At least, that's what the locals say. Of course, the beams just may not have been properly seasoned when the tower was built. Violet Pinwell's carvings are found in churches all over Devon. She began her carving here, where she was the daughter of the vicar.

Ermington used to be an important market place where the main road between Plymouth and Totnes crossed the River Erme. In the early 1900s it was planned to put it on the railway network and the three storey cottages near the start of this walk were built to house the intended railway's workers.

As well as a slate water trough and pump, the foot of Town Hill boasts the old toll house. This hexagonally-shaped building gave the toll collector a good view of the important turnpike road between Plymouth and Totnes.

The Crooked Spire Inn

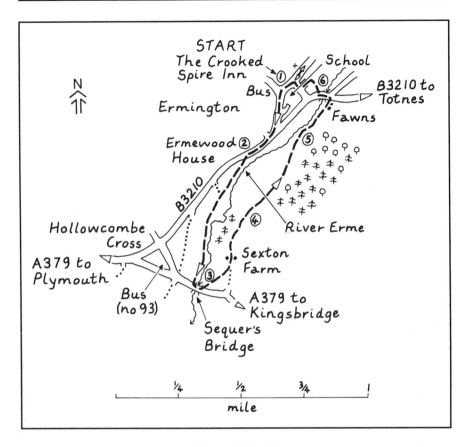

The Walk

1. Go down Town Hill, passing the Post Office on your right. Pass a slate water trough and pump on your right at its foot. Turn right along the A3121.

2. Bear left along the signposted public footpath which leads to the river and, eventually, to Sequer's Bridge. Cross the bridge by road.

3. Bear left over a stile to follow the signposted path diagonally across the field to Sexton Farm. Follow the waymarked path through the farmyard and go ahead through a gate to take a hedged track waymarked as part of the Erme Valley Trail.

4. Continue over a stile and with a hedge on your left to a stile ahead, near the corner of a wood on your right. Go ahead through a gap near the next corner of this wood and reach the river.

5. Go ahead over a series of stiles and gates, keeping the River Erme on your left. Reach the A3121 and turn left with this road across a bridge.

6. Bear right across the village playing fields, then turn left along Fawns Close and right up Bunkers Hill, passing the school on your left. Divert right to visit the Church of St Peter and St Paul (and of the Crooked Spire) before returning to the centre of the village and the pub.

18. Loddiswell

Route: Loddiswell – The Primrose Line – Avon Mill – Loddiswell

Distance: $3^1/_2$ miles (plus an optional 2 miles to Loddiswell Vineyard and back)

Map: O.S. Outdoor Leisure 20 South Devon

Start: The Loddiswell Inn (Grid Reference SX 720486)

Access: Bus no 162 runs to Loddiswell from Kingsbridge (the service is better on Fridays). There is also the X65 bus (Salcombe – Kingsbridge – Loddiswell – Exeter) on Saturdays

The Loddiswell Inn (0548 550308)

The ghost of a lady dressed in grey haunts the foot of the steps leading from the bar to the restaurant, while the ghost of an old man has been seen sitting in the corner near the fire. Investigate these at your leisure by staying in the pub's self-catering flat. Real ale is served, while the food includes vegetarian fare. Formerly an old coaching inn called the Turk's Head, this pub used to cater for prisoners on their way to Dartmoor. Opening hours are 11.30 am to 2.30 pm and 6 pm to 11 pm on weekdays, noon to 3 pm and 7 pm to 10.30 pm on Sundays.

The Primrose Line

Running between the main Great Western line at South Brent and Kingsbridge, this was one of the country's most beautiful railways. First mooted in the 1860s, it wasn't built until 1893. It closely followed the winding River Avon and led through delightful woods. From February to May you could enjoy a visual feast of flowers out of the carriage window, with snowdrops, wild daffodils, wood anemones, bluebells and marsh marigolds. Above all, there were the primroses In March. The shortsighted Dr Beeching took his scalpel to this route in 1963, but you can still enjoy the flowers by walking the course of the dismantled railway in due season.

Loddiswell Vineyard

If you have time extend this walk to visit Loddiswell Vineyard. This is open between 1 pm and 6 pm from Monday to Friday (and on Sundays in July and August) and on Bank Holiday Sundays between Easter and October 31st. Taste three award-winning English wines made with local grapes that have been fermented in the modern winery. Guided tours are available, while wine can be purchased from the shop.

Avon Mill

Near the end of the walk, the Mill Coffee Shop is well-situated to cater for hungry ramblers. The cakes are homemade and scrumptious. Housed in a corner of an old Corn Mill within the grounds of a Nursery and Garden Centre, it is open from 10.30 am to 5 pm on weekdays, 2 pm to 5 pm on Sundays.

The Walk

1. Go right and turn right along the main road through Loddiswell. Pass the sports ground on your left and a lane to Ham Butts on your right. Pass Loddiswell Butts road junction on your left, then an access lane to Ham Farm on your right.

2. Turn right along a signed public footpath. It may look overgrown, but venture between its hedgerows and it becomes an enjoyable path which descends to woodland. Bear left to step across a stream.

3. Cross the River Avon by an old railway bridge and turn right along the trackbed of the old railway. Go through woodland and above the river on your right.

4. As the path approaches a gate ahead, turn left over a waymarked

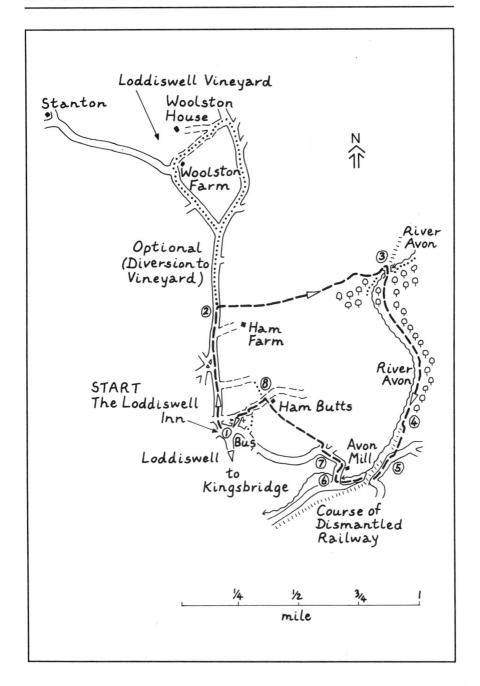

Stanton

Loddiswell Vineyard
Woolston
House

Woolston
Farm

N

Optional
(Diversion to
Vineyard)

River
Avon

③

②

Ham
Farm

River
Avon

START
The Loddiswell
Inn

⑧ Ham Butts

④

① Bus

Loddiswell

Avon
Mill

to
Kingsbridge

⑦

⑤

⑥

Course of
Dismantled
Railway

¼   ½   ¾   1

mile

stile and turn right immediately to follow a narrow path to a road, with the course of the dismantled railway on your right. Climb a stile at the end to reach the road at the old Loddiswell Station.

5. Go right down a road (ignore a track bearing right to Rake Farm). Bear right at a crossroads to go under an old railway bridge. Take a gate in the hedge on your right to follow a meadow path beside the river on your right.

6. Turn right across the road bridge over the river. Pass Avon Mill Garden Centre, Coffee Shop and Sleepy Hollow Gallery of Rural Crafts on your right. Continue uphill to a junction with tracks on your right.

7. Bear right up a track and soon turn left to follow the hedged track to the crossroads at Ham Butts.

8. Turn left, as signposted for Loddiswell. This roughly-metalled lane passes St Michael and All Angels Church on your left. Fork left to reach the centre of the village and its pub.

Loddiswell Inn

19. Dartmouth

Route: Dartmouth – Dartmouth Castle – Blackstone Point – Warren Point – Little Dartmouth – Dartmouth

Distance: $5^1/_2$ miles

Map: O.S. Outdoor Leisure 20 South Devon

Start: The Dartmouth Arms (Grid Reference SX 878511)

Access: Dartmouth is a short ferry-ride from the southern terminus of the Dart Valley Railway (connecting with British Rail at Paignton) at Kingswear. Ferries come down the River Dart from Totnes and bus no 89 also links Totnes with Dartmouth. Bus no 93 comes from Plymouth. Why not buy a Round Robin ticket for a road-rail-river tour on the Totnes – Paignton – Dartmouth circuit?

The Dartmouth Arms
(0803 832903)

Agincourt House (which dates from the 14th century) next door has two ghosts, but they don't appear to need refreshment in this pub. *The Mayflower* set out from here in 1620 and the original passenger list is on display. Real ale and food are served, with pizzas a speciality. Opening hours are 11 am to 11 pm on weekdays, noon to 3 pm and 7 pm to 10.30 pm on Sundays.

Dartmouth

The narrow streets exude history, while the Britannia Royal Naval College cements the port's link with the navy. An international fleet of 164 ships assembled here for the Second Crusade in 1147, while part of Richard the Lionheart's Third Crusade fleet sailed from here in 1190. Later the town flourished from the trade of English wool for Bordeaux wine. Geoffrey Chaucer's 'Shipman' in his *Canterbury Tales* came from Dartmouth. He stole wine from his master and made enemies walk the plank. Bayard's Cove has changed little since its castle was built by Henry VIII in 1539. The Custom House was built in the 18th century.

Dartmouth Castle

This occupies a superb defensive position, jutting out into the narrow entrance to the Dart estuary and with the sea lapping its feet. It was the first English Castle to be built with artillery in mind, being started in 1481. There is a Victorian battery with a full equipment of guns. In the care of English Heritage, it is open daily from April to September between 10 am and 6 pm. From October to March it is open between Tuesday and Sunday from 10 am to 4 pm (closed from 24th to 26th December and on 1st January).

The Walk

1. Go right to walk with the harbour on your left to Bayard's Cove Fort. Go through to its far end and turn right up steps to the road. Turn left to walk above the Dart Estuary on your left. Bear left at a fork to follow Warfleet Road, then fork left along Castle Road and fork left along the lower road to visit Dartmouth Castle.

2. Climb steps to the higher road and fork left to pass the picnic place on your left. Descend steps and follow the cliff path below trees. Go down to Sugary Cove then climb the path which zigzags through woodland. Bear left at a junction.

3. Follow a lane briefly, then fork left to take the signposted Coast Path towards Little Dartmouth.

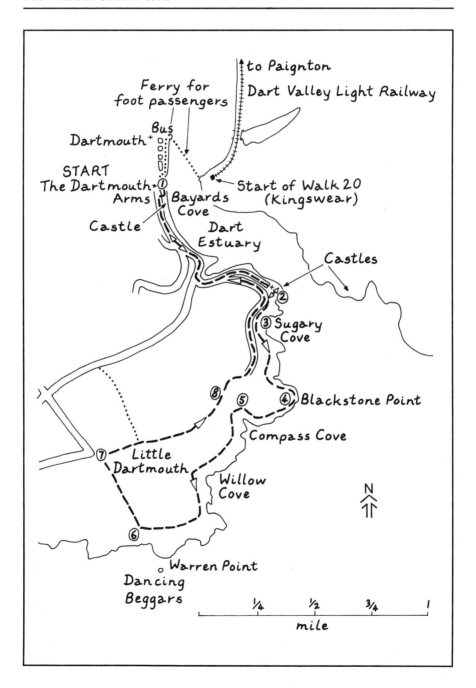

to Paignton

Dart Valley Light Railway

Ferry for
foot passengers

Bus

Dartmouth

START
The Dartmouth
Arms

Bayards
Cove

Start of Walk 20
(Kingswear)

Castle

Dart
Estuary

Castles

②

③ Sugary
Cove

⑧ ⑤ ④ Blackstone Point

Compass Cove

⑦ Little
Dartmouth

Willow
Cove

⑥

N

Warren Point

Dancing
Beggars

¼   ½   ¾   1

mile

4. Continue downhill to Blackstone Point and walk close to the sea. Cross a footbridge over a narrow inlet and climb above Compass Cove (which it is worth diverting into).

5. Follow the waymarked Coast Path, taking a gate and passing a stile on your right before crossing another stile. The clifftop path leads to a small footbridge. Continue around a hill and take a gap in a wall to turn right and walk beside it.

6. Turn right, inland, with a fence. Take a kissing-gate and go along the left-hand edges of fields to reach a National Trust car park.

7. Go right, along the signposted bridleway for Dartmouth. After Little Dartmouth this becomes a muddy, hedged, track. Continue over a stile and along the blue-waymarked bridleway.

8. Continue along the road from the old coastguard's cottages. Follow it all the way back to Dartmouth and the Dartmouth Arms at Bayard's Cove.

20. Kingswear

Route: Kingswear – Brownstone Fort – High Brownstone – Kingswear

Distance: 5 miles

Map: O.S. Outdoor Leisure 20 South Devon

Start: Royal Dart Bars (Grid Reference SX 882510)

Access: Kingswear is the southern terminus of the Dart Valley Railway. This links with British Rail at Paignton. Bus no 22 comes from Brixham. Otherwise, the ferry from Dartmouth can bring you from buses and ferries to that town (see Walk 19).

Royal Dart Bars (0803 752213)

This pub couldn't be more convenient for trains and ferries! Real ale and food are served. Opening hours are 11 am to 11 pm on weekdays, noon to 3 pm and 7 pm to 10.30 pm on Sundays.

The Dart Valley Railway

Take a nostalgic journey into the days of the Great Western Railway when you ride behind a steam locomotive on this scenic line. It was an extension to the main line to Torre from Newton Abbot and when work started on it in 1857 the intention was to build a bridge to a terminus in Dartmouth. Permission to bridge the estuary was refused, so when trains terminated at Kingswear in 1864, ferries maintained the final connection. Excessive pruning led British Rail to lop off the route south of Paignton. It kept going without a break, however, by being taken over as a private, steam-hauled, line by the Dart Valley Light Railway Ltd, in 1972. The world-famous L.N.E.R. locomotive *Flying Scotsman* made its first successful season on it in 1973. The service is seasonal, from April to October plus Santa Steam Specials before Christmas. Telephone 0803 555872 for full details.

A former GWR locomotive at Kingswear station

The Daymark

Marked on the map as The Tower (Day Beacon) this is 80 foot high and was built in 1864 as a navigational aid.

'H' Jones

The memorial plaque to Lt. Col. H. Jones, VC, OBE, was unveiled by his widow in July, 1984. After his death in the Falklands War in 1982, it was agreed to open a new length of the Coast Path from Kingswear Castle to Newfoundland Cove in his memory. 'H' Jones had close family links with this area.

The Walk

1. Go left above the station and turn sharply right as signed for the library to pass Kingswear Hall (opened on 4th July, 1925) and the Church of St Thomas of Canterbury (c1170) on your left. Climb past a signposted public footpath down steps to the estuary on your right. Ignore a hairpin bend and a fork ahead on your left (Ridley Hill/ Castle Road). Take Beacon Lane ahead.

2. Reach a signposted path junction and a memorial plaque to the Falklands War hero Lieutenant Colonel Herbert ('H') Jones VC OBE. Turn right down the Coast Path (wooden steps initially) and reach a signposted junction at Brownstone Fort.

3. Turn left to Brownstone Car Park, following a firm lane. Divert right over a stile to The Daymark (a tower). Resume your former path, going inland.

4. Fork left down the signposted path for Kingswear. Reach a lane and turn left to pass High Brownstone on your right and farm buildings on your left. Descend past Crockers Cottage on your right and go down a narrow, hedged, path.

5. Emerge onto a lane at Home Farm and go left along it.

6. Fork left down the waymarked Coast Path. Pass steps on your right. Reach the road opposite the church and go left back down to the pub.

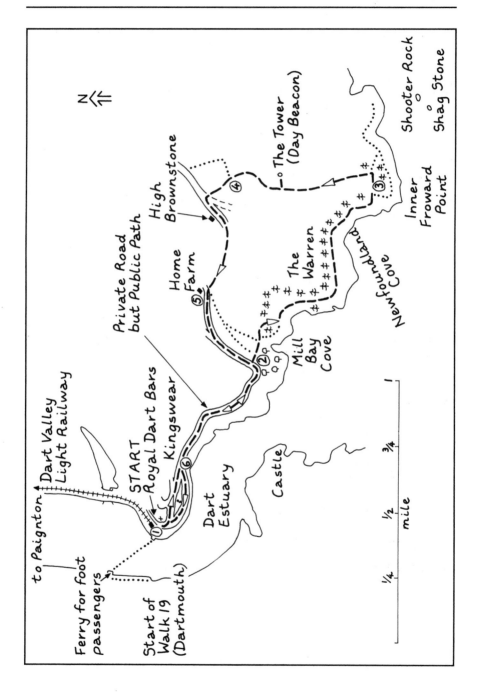

N

to Paignton

Ferry for foot Passengers

Dart Valley Light Railway

Start of Walk 19 (Dartmouth)

START Royal Dart Bars Kingswear

Dart Estuary

Castle

Private Road but Public Path

High Brownstone

Home Farm

The Warren

Mill Bay Cove

Newfoundland

The Tower (Day Beacon)

Shooter Rock

Shag Stone

Inner Froward Point

¼   ½   ¾
     mile

21. Noss Mayo

Route: Noss Mayo – Mouth Stone Point – Warren Cottage – Noss Mayo

Distance: 4 miles

Map: O.S. Pathfinder 1362 Newton Ferrers

Start: The Old Ship Inn (Grid Reference SX 548477)

Access: Bus no 94 runs from Plymouth to Noss Mayo on weekdays.

The Old Ship Inn (0752 872387)

This 16th century pub used to be a smugglers' den, although it was originally a bonded warehouse. George the Ghost is often heard walking through the dining room at night. There is a lovely terrace overlooking the harbour where you can enjoy your real ale and food. Opening hours are 11 am to 3.30 pm and 6 pm to 11 pm, noon to 3 pm and 7 pm to 10.30 pm on Sundays.

The Old Ship

Revelstoke Drive

The Coast Path follows a relaxing route between the former Coastguard Station and Warren Cottage. This 19th century carriage drive was cut by Lord Revelstoke to enable his guests to admire his estate from the comfort of his carriage. It makes an excellent walk, affording views of the Great Mew Stone, a steep-sided off-shore islet which forms part of the H.M.S. *Cambridge* gunnery school at Wembury Point. Warren Cottage housed the warrener above gently sloping cliffs near Blackstone Point where rabbits were bred for their flesh and skins.

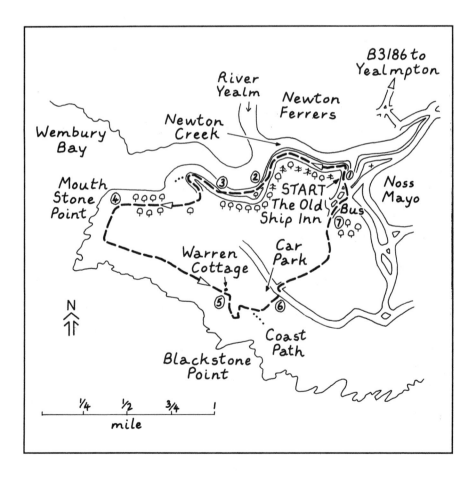

The Walk

1. Facing the harbour, turn left to take steps to the road. Go right along the road above the harbour on your right. Follow the road as it bends left. Newton Ferrers is across the creek on your right.

2. Fork right along the signposted Coast Path and fork right again when you are above an old ferry slip. Pass Ferryman's Cottage on your right and take a kissing-gate ahead to follow a delightful woodland walk.

3. Rejoin the lane and bear right along it. Ignore a waymarked path on your right and follow the lane as it bears left at Battery Cottages to reach the former Coastguard Station. Continue along a firm track which bears right through Brakehill Plantation.

4. Bear left with the track around Mouthstone Point, keeping the sea on your right. The little, rocky, island is Great Mew Stone.

5. Follow the signposted Coast Path to pass below Warren Cottage. Ignore the Coast Path when it forks right at the next signpost. Bear inland with the firm track to pass a car park on your left and reach a lane.

6. Go left along the lane for 30 yards then turn right down a firm track signposted as the public footpath to Noss Mayo.

7. As you enter Noss Mayo, take the metalled lane past the playground and car park on your right. Reach the bus stop and bear left to follow the road down to the harbour and the Old Ship Inn.

22. Bantham

Route: Bantham – Bantham Sand – Thurleston – Bantham

Distance: $3^1/_2$ miles

Map: O.S. Pathfinder 1362 Newton Ferrers

Start: The Sloop Inn (Grid Reference SX 669437)

Access: Bus no 161 runs to Bantham from Kingsbridge on Wednesdays only. If you can't make a Wednesday, bus no 162 from Kingsbridge stops at Thurleston Church on Fridays.

The Sloop Inn (0548 560489)

This pub was once owned by John Whiddon, one of Devon's most notorious smugglers and wreckers. Ask the landlady to point out the places in the village where the kegs of brandy were hidden. One of the bars is made from old boat-timbers, while the low beams and stone-flagged floors add to the atmosphere. The food is home-cooked and delicious, including a choice of at least six vegetarian dishes each day. Bed and breakfast and self-catering accommodation are available, as is real ale. Open-

ing hours are 11 am to 2.30 pm and 6 pm to 11 pm on weekdays, noon
to 2.30 pm and 7 pm to 10.30 pm on Sundays.

Thurlestone Church

All Saints Church, Thurlestone, has a Lady Chapel with carved frag-
ments from an ancient rood screen. The font dates from the 12th century.
Tubs of brandy used to be hidden on the church roof by smugglers with
the compliance of the rector until the anti-smuggling Rev. Peregrine
Ilbert came in 1839.

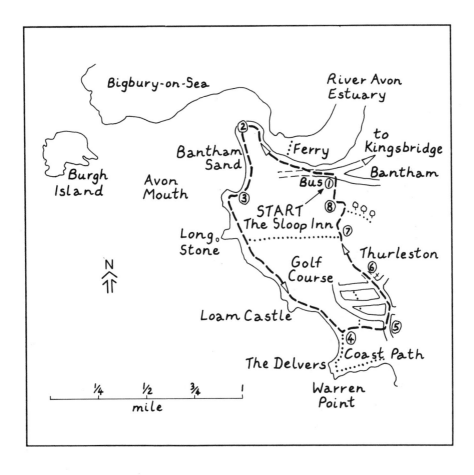

The Walk

1. Go left down the road to the bus turning bay. Go ahead through a kissing-gate and fork right to follow the Coast Path above the estuary of the River Avon, on your right.

2. Keep to the Coast Path as it bears left to pass above Bantham Sand on your right. Burgh Island is off-shore on the far side of the estuary mouth. Cross the sand dunes or, at low tide, the beach to Bantham Surf Life Saving Club's building.

3. Go ahead over a stile and bear right along the signposted Coast Path to Thurlestone. Walk with the sea on your right and notice the isolated Long Stone at the end of a promontory. Continue over a stile to follow the clifftop path past a golf course on your left and above a beach on your right.

4. Turn left along the signposted public footpath inland across the golf course. Do not go through the small gate ahead. Turn right to walk with a wall and houses on your left to reach a road.

5. Go left along the road until it bends right at Thurlestone's war memorial. Take the signposted track ahead to pass All Saints Church on your right.

6. Take the gate ahead to continue along the right-hand edge of a field. Cross a stile in the corner ahead to continue walking parallel to a fence on your left and go over a stile in the wall ahead. Pass the golf course on your left.

7. Ignore the stile on your left in the corner. Take the stile ahead and go down sloping pasture to cross a stile in a lower hedge. Bear slightly right to descend to a stile in the bottom right-hand corner. Cross it to descend to the floor of this valley, then bear left to where a corner juts out.

8. Turn right to go up an enclosed path. Emerge in Bantham at the side of the Sloop Inn, which is on your left.

The enclosed path to the Sloop Inn

23. Kingsbridge

Route: Kingsbridge – Easton – West Alvington – Kingsbridge

Distance: $3^1/_2$ miles

Map: O.S. Outdoor Leisure 20 South Devon

Start: The Ship and Plough Inn (Grid Reference SX 735441)

Access: Buses to Kingsbridge include the no 93 (Plymouth – Kingsbridge – Dartmouth) and no 164 (from Totnes, where there is a railway station)

The Ship and Plough Inn (0548 852485)

This pub opens to a tremendous view of the estuary, which used to come just that bit further inland to make it a convenient place for ships. Built as a coaching inn in 1794, the large stables now house a restaurant. The pub brews its own real ale (Blewitt's Best Bitter and Brains Out). Opening hours are 11 am to 11 pm on weekdays, noon to 3 pm and 7 pm to 10.30 pm on Sundays.

Kingsbridge

Nothing is known of the original King's Bridge but a bridge here at the head of the tidal estuary would have linked two royal estates in the 10th century. Its market was established by monks in 1219. Later, in the 18th century, its port became important for lime, burnt in kilns and distributed to surrounding farmland.

The Quay, Kingsbridge

West Alvington

All Saints Church dates from at least 909 AD. In the churchyard, at the east end, can be seen the unusual headstone of Daniel Jeffrey and Joan his wife. 'He was buried ye 2 day of September 1746 in ye 18th year of his age. This youth when in sickness lay did for the minister send that he would come and with him pray but he would not attend. But when this young man buried was the minister did him admit he should be carried into church that he might money geet. By this you see what man will dwo to geet money if he can, who did refuse to come and pray by the forsaid young man'.

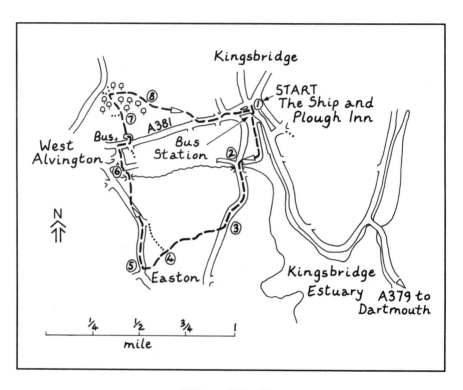

The Walk

1. Go left and take a zebra crossing on your right to reach the bus station and Tourist Information Centre. Walk beside the harbour with the water on your left to reach a slipway ahead. Bear right up steps and take a well-trodden path across a field, keeping above a creek on your left. Reach a road near a T-junction.

2. Go left with the road across a bridge. Pass Sandy Park on your left.

3. Turn right over a stile to take a signposted public footpath. Cross the brow of a hill to converge with a hedge coming from your right. When the hedge turns right, go ahead to the left of the TV mast on the horizon. Descend to a gate in the corner formed by a fence on your left and a hedge on your right.

4. Go through the gate and immediately turn right over a stile. Immediately turn left over a second stile to enter another field. Descend with a hedge on your left to its corner. Keeping in the same field, turn right to follow the hedge on your left until a gate in it. Bear left through this down to a road.

5. Turn right up the road. When the road descends, look for an opening on your right through which you bear right to cross a stile and go downhill with West Alvington Church ahead across the valley. Take a stile in the bottom fence and cross a narrow field to a stile beside a gate. Bear left up to a stile in the top corner.

6. Go up a road, passing Feoffees Cottage on your right. Reach the A381 below the church and turn right along its pavement. Pass a telephone box on your left and turn left up a lane which bears left at its end. Turn right up an old green lane to a stile giving admission to woods.

7. Turn right at the start of the woods and descend to a stile beside a gate in their bottom left corner. Do not go onto the road! Turn right along the lower path through the woods. Take a stile out of the woods to follow their edge on your right. Cross a stile in a fence ahead.

8. Take the well-trodden path diverging from the woods. Go ahead over a stile to follow an old green lane to a road. Turn left along its pavement to a roundabout and bear right down to the town centre and the Ship and Plough.

24. Slapton

Route: Slapton – Boardwalk – Lower Green Cross – Slapton

Distance: $2^1/_2$ miles

Map: O.S. Outdoor Leisure 20 South Devon

Start: The Queen's Arms (Grid Reference SX 821449)

Access: Bus no 93 links Slapton with Dartmouth and Plymouth (via Kingsbridge). Be warned! Most services do not enter the village but run past the monument beside the A379 near the beach

The Queen's Arms (0548 580800)

Local farm cider, real ale and food (including vegetarian fare) are served in this very old pub. The present building dates from the 15th century. Opening hours are 11.30 am to 3 pm and 6 pm to 11 pm on weekdays, noon to 3 pm and 7 pm to 10.30 pm on Saturdays.

The Tower Inn (0548 580216)

There has been a pub here since at least the 1370s. Sir Guy de Brien, Lord of the

Manor and Steward to Edward III, founded a college of chantry priests next door in 1373. This pub housed the workmen who built its chantry tower. The (friendly) ghost of a monk wanders around the pub. The U.S. army found accommodation here in 1943/44 when they took over the area in preparation for D Day. Stay for bed and breakfast, sample a meal or simply linger outside with a jar of real ale. Opening hours are 11.30 am to 3 pm and 6 pm to 11 pm on weekdays, noon to 3 pm and 7 pm to 10.30 pm on Sundays.

Slapton

Certain seemingly insignificant villages have a special feel to them that soon makes the visitor realise he or she is walking on hallowed ground. The parish church is usually a good place to start an enquiry into the nature of a village and the Church of St James the Great is found to offer sanctuary. A big ring on its door (inside the northern porch) should be touched by those who need to escape earthly justice. After making a full confession, the penitents were allowed to take the shortest route out of the realm and the jurisdiction of its courts. Sir Guy de Brien, who had the chantry tower built, must have had a lot to repent for, otherwise why did he invest in the chantry with its four priests bound to ensure that the mass was said for Sir Guy's soul in perpetuity? He got 174 years' worth for his money. The tower no doubt occupies a sacred spot and tunnel legends abound at such places. In this case there is truth in them, with a tunnel starting from under a nearby bush and leading to the sea. The tower and the tunnel entrance are on private land, so don't go investigating without permission. No doubt the tunnel was used by smugglers. The tower was where, it is said, Eisenhower stayed when in the area preparing for D Day. The whole village and surrounding areas were evacuated in December 1943, so that Slapton Sands could be used as a mock-up of the ·Normandy beaches for live-ammo battle practices. The memorial near the bus stop on the A379 was erected by the Americans to thank all those villagers who had to be evacuated from their homes in the area for the exercises. Slapton is now invaded by student biologists and other naturalists who visit the Field Studies Centre. They come for Slapton Ley which is featured in Walk 26 (Torcross). This route shares the exciting boardwalk with it, giving you two opportunities to tread its boards!

The Chantry Tower

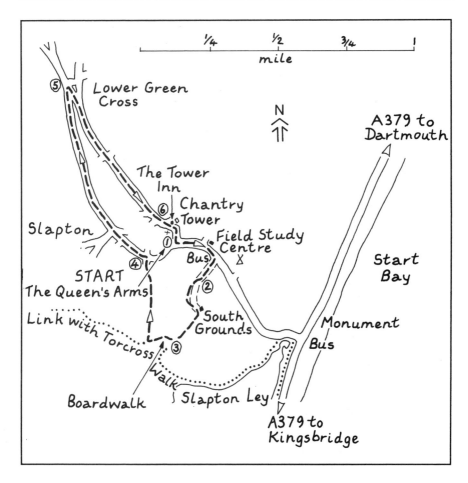

The Walk

1. Go right and turn left. Pass the bus shelter on your right and the Field Study Centre on your left. Turn right through a gate to follow the access lane to Southgrounds Farm. This is signposted as a public footpath.

2. Bear right over a stile beside a gate to follow the signposted footpath which runs between a pond on your left and a marshy arm of Slapton Ley on your right. Bear right, as signposted, when you reach a corner.

3. Go over a stile beside a gate and join the route of Walk 26 (Torcross) for a few yards by turning right along the signposted boardwalk. When you reach firm ground again, fork right along the signposted path into Slapton, passing a plant nursery on your right.

4. Go left along the road out of the village for about one mile.

5. Turn sharply right at Lower Green Cross to return to Slapton a different way.

6. Look for the entrance to the Tower Inn on your left, pass the Chantry Tower on your left and the church on your right. Continue to the Queen's Arms, on your right.

25. Frogmore

Route: Frogmore – Frogmore Creek – West Charleton – Frogmore

Distance: 5 miles

Map: O.S. Outdoor Leisure 20 South Devon

Start: The Globe Inn (Grid Reference SX 775426)

Access: Bus no 93 (Plymouth – Kingsbridge – Dartmouth) stops in both Frogmore and West Charleton

The Globe Inn (0548 531351)

The ale is real and the food is varied with some dishes vegetarian at this pub which also offers bed and breakfast accommodation. Built in the 18th century as a pub and a carpenter's workshop, it is said to be haunted by a ghost who consumes breakfasts that are laid out on tables overnight. The fireplace in the lounge is made of gravestones. Opening hours are 11 am to 3 pm and 5.30 pm to 11 pm on weekdays, noon to 3 pm and 7 pm to 10.30 pm on Sundays.

Frogmore

Sailing boats of up to 100 tons used to reach the head of this creek. Coal wharves and corn stores still stood here in the 19th century. Geese Quarries produced slate and stone from which West Charleton church and Dartmouth Castle were built in the 15th century.

The Globe Inn

The Walk

1. Go right and look for a public footpath signpost on your left. Turn left between two houses to take it to a fieldgate. Go ahead down the left-hand side of a field towards Frogmore Creek. Turn right in the bottom corner to walk with the creek on your left.

2. Go ahead over a stone step stile to follow the path above the creek on your left. Emerge over another stile into a field and go ahead along its edge, above the creek. Take a stile into the next field and bear right to a farm building. Turn left to go through a gate and pass a small islet on your left.

3. Walk with the creek on your left as you go over a series of stiles (five in all) before following the path through a scrubby area and a patch of woodland to a signpost on the beach. Continue past the creek on your left for 400 yards.

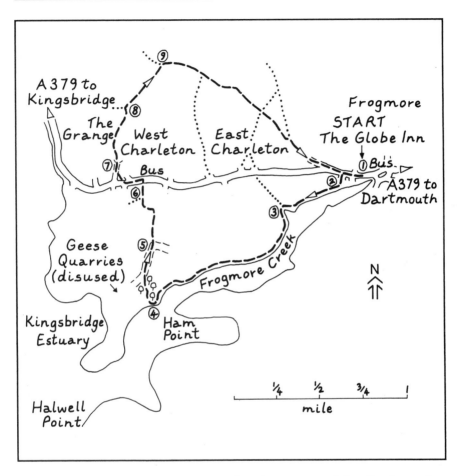

4. Bear right at a track and pass a bench on your right. Go through a gate at the top and along a firm, hedged, lane which has come from old quarries on your left.

5. When the lane turns right take a signposted footpath through a gate ahead and go straight down a field towards West Charleton. Reach the bottom hedge and turn left along the headland path until you come to a stile on your right. Cross it and a subsequent small footbridge and a stile into the next field. Go ahead as directed by a yellow arrow, bearing slightly left to pass a duckpond on your right.

6. Go ahead over a stile to emerge from between two houses on the main road. Go left to pass the Ashburton Arms on your right. 100 yards after it, turn right up a signposted public footpath. This leads to a lane.

7. Turn right up the lane and reach a fork. Go ahead, between the two prongs of the fork, to cross a stile and enter a field. Walk with a hedge on your left, continue through a gate and bear right to a gate in the hedge ahead. Walk past Charleton Grange across the valley on your left. Cross a stone step stile in the wall at the far end of this field. Descend gradually to a stream on your left.

8. Cross the stream where it is bridged near a signpost and turn right to walk with it on your right, going upstream. Continue through a gate, up a long field to a stone step stile beside a signpost and to the left of a gate in the far corner ahead.

9. Go right along a delightful old green lane. Pass two turnings on your right. Eventually join a track coming from your left and turn right downhill to Frogmore. Go left to return to the Globe Inn.

26. Torcross

Route: Torcross – Slapton Ley – Deer Bridge – Frittiscombe – Stokenham – Torcross

Distance: $6^1/_2$ miles

Map: O.S. Outdoor Leisure 20 South Devon

Start: Start Bay Inn (Grid Reference SX 823422)

Access: Start Bay is on the route of the no 93 bus, which also stops at Slapton Turn and Stokenham on its way between Dartmouth and Plymouth (via Kingsbridge)

Start Bay Inn (0548 580553)

The landlord's mother has seen the ghost of a little girl dressed in Victorian clothes here. Ask her about it. Local seafood is a speciality in this pub which dates back to the 17th century (the pub that is, not the seafood). Real ale is served and the opening hours are 11.30 am to 2.30 pm and 6 pm to 11 pm on weekdays, noon to 3 pm and 7 pm to 10.30 pm on Sundays.

The Tradesman's Arms, Stokenham (0548 580313)

The 'nicest French onion soup in the world' and a special Madras curry are highly recommended in this very friendly pub. The traditionally brewed ale is good too (Adnams). The building began life as cottages in the late 14th century and was known as a pub in the 16th century. Opening hours are noon to 2.30 pm daily, 7 pm to 11 pm on weekdays, 7 pm to 10.30 pm on Sundays.

Church House Inn, Stokenham (0548 580253)

This building dates from the 16th century, but there has been a pub here for almost as long as a church has stood across the road (since the 10th century at least). Real ale and food are served, with local seafood a speciality. Opening hours are 11 am to 11 pm on weekdays, noon to 3 pm and 7 pm to 10.30 pm on Sundays.

The Village Inn, Torcross (0548 580206)

Bed and breakfast accommodation is available at this pub. Built in 1894, it has seen Molly Sugden (the actress in *Are you being served?*), Lesley Thomas and U.S. army generals accept its hospitality. The food includes vegetarian choices, while real ale is served. Opening hours are 11 am to 11 pm on weekdays, noon to 3 pm and 7 pm to 10.30 pm on Sundays.

A Major Disaster

Slapton Sands (actually a shingle ridge) was commandeered for training the U.S. army in preparation for the invasion of France in 1944. It was selected to represent Utah Beach. Live ammunition was used in Operation Tiger, the rehearsal for D-Day, with many soldiers losing their lives. The worst tragedy was suffered on the night of 27th April, 1944, when German E-boats came across some all-too-lightly-defended ships in the Channel. Two were sunk with the loss of nearly 1000 American servicemen, including 749 soldiers. The incoming tide bore the bodies to Torcross and the truth was concealed. Only after 6th June were the families of the dead men informed, and then that they had died in the real D-Day landings. The Sherman tank you see on this walk was not involved in the tragedy. Its waterproof 'skirt' was damaged whilst taking part in another exercise. This caused it to sink when it was launched into the water from the tank landing craft. All the crew managed to escape and the tank was later salvaged (from a depth of 60 feet). It was placed in its present position by a team of divers from Fort Bovisand, Plymouth (see Walk 15). Bought from the U.S. government, it now serves as a memorial to the men who died.

Slapton Ley

This remarkable freshwater lake is a Site of Special Scientific Interest. The reeds and marshes are home to otters and birds such as reed warblers and water rails. Hundreds of gulls roost here.

The Walk

1. Walk with the sea on your right and the A379 road on your left for a few yards, until the far end of the car park across the road. Turn left across the road carefully and go right to take the footpath between the road and Slapton Ley (the freshwater lake). After about one and a half miles reach the road which goes left to Slapton. Turn left with it to cross a bridge.

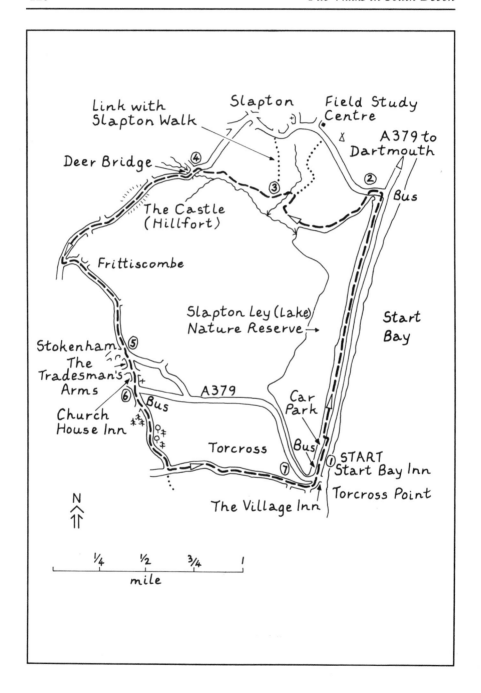

2. Bear left down a signposted footpath, going through a wooden gate. Take the nature trail beside the lake on your left. Reach a signpost where this route links with Walk 24 (Slapton). Turn left along the boardwalk over a marshy arm of Slapton Ley.

3. Fork left, as signposted for Deer Bridge.

4. Go left down a road and bear left at a junction to cross Deer Bridge. Follow the road uphill. Pass Fittiscombe Lodge on your left and turn left along a quiet lane.

5. Turn at a junction with Kiln Lane and almost immediately turn left downhill. Turn right at the next T-junction to reach the Tradesman's Arms, continue straight ahead to pass St Michael's Church on your left and reach Church House Inn, Stokenham, on your right.

6. Go ahead up the lane opposite (cross the A379 carefully). Turn left at a T-junction along a lane to Torcross.

7. Pass a viewpoint on your left (with a notice board detailing 20 species of local butterflies). Pass the Village Inn on your right as you bear left to reach Start Bay Inn on your right. The Sherman tank is on your left.

27. Salcombe

Route: Salcombe – Ferry – Mill Bay – Coast Path – Garn Rock Hotel – Mill Bay – Ferry – Salcombe

Distance: 5 miles

Map: O.S. Outdoor Leisure 20 South Devon or O.S. Pathfinder 1367 Salcombe

Start: The Fortescue Inn (Grid Reference SX 741392)

Access: If you're travelling on a Western National day rover ticket, come to Salcombe on a Saturday from Kingsbridge on bus no X65, or on Mondays and Thursdays during school terms or on Thursdays only during school summer holidays from Kingsbridge on bus no X92. Salcombe does have a much better bus service than that if you forget about Western National's rovers. Tally Ho! Service no 606 runs regularly between Kingsbridge and Salcombe every weekday.

The Fortescue Inn (0548 842868)

The charm of Salcombe's narrow streets complements the colourful boats and yachts in its harbour. It is both busy and relaxed and here, at its heart, is The Fortescue. You may find yourself sharing the beer garden with a TV personality. The 17th century building is open for breakfasts from 8 am, with the bar open between 11 am and 11 pm on weekdays, from noon to 3 pm and 7 pm to 10.30 pm on Sundays. Real ale and food are served by the most cheerful of staff.

Gara Rock Hotel (0548 842342/1)

Built as coastguard cottages in 1847, this became a hotel in 1909 (and retained the thatched coastguard lookout). The bar is open to non-residents between 11 am and 2.30 pm on weekdays (noon to 2.30 pm on Sundays). Food and real ale are available. Why not stay here on a self-catering basis?

The Fortescue

Salcombe

Its name, 'Salt Combe', is apt because Salcombe is not on a freshwater estuary but a saltwater ria (a drowned river valley). The port also has a mild climate, reflecting its southerly position. Salcombe's history doesn't really begin until the 19th century, however, when it built schooners that raced back from the West Indies, Azores or Mediterranean with fruit. Tourists also started to come in great numbers after the railway reached Kingsbridge in 1893. Henry VIII did deem the harbour worth defending with a castle. This finally saw action in the Civil War when it became the last fortress in England to hold out for Charles I. Its commander was Sir Edmund Fortescue, who spent £3,000 of his own money on repairs, renamed the castle Fort Charles and withstood a Roundhead siege begun by General Fairfax in January, 1646. Parliamentary cannon finally forced surrender on honourable terms to Colonel Weldon, the governor of Plymouth, on 3rd June, 1646. Two washerwomen were among the 66 strong garrison that was granted leave to march out bearing arms and with colours flying. It then became one of those castles that 'Cromwell knocked about a bit' and is virtually demolished.

The Bar is across the mouth of Salcombe Harbour and its sands are a trap for deep-keeled craft at low tide. Thirteen of Salcombe lifeboat's crew of fifteen were drowned when it was lost here in October, 1916. Shipwrecks have been fairly common along this stretch of coastline, with one wreck to the east of Gara Rock believed to date from the Bronze Age.

The Walk

1. Go right and turn left along Fore Street. Turn left down steps between Salcombe Hotel and the Midland Bank for the ferry, which you take across Salcombe Harbour.

2. Climb steps from the ferry to a lane and turn right along it to pass the beach at Mill Bay on your right.

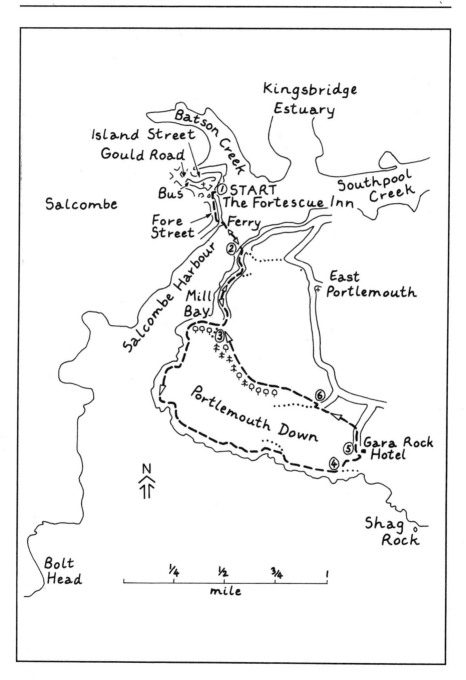

3. Bear right along a woodland path which is signposted as the Coast Path to Gara Rock (2$^1/_4$ miles). Follow it around Portlemouth Down above the sea on your right.

4. Look up to see an old, thatched, coastguard lookout and fork left up past it to the Gara Rock Hotel, which was built as coastguard cottages in 1847. Turn left, as signposted for Mill Bay.

5. Go right, through the hotel car park, to follow a lane. Turn left over a stile beside a small gate and take the path ahead to a stile in the hedge opposite. Continue through the next field to a stile beside a gate. Continue along a shaded path to emerge through a gate onto a muddy lane.

6. Turn right and immediately turn left to take the lower old green lane which soon runs beside woodland on your left back down to Mill Bay. Go right to retrace your steps to the ferry, Salcombe and the pub.

Opposite: Looking east from the Gara Rock Hotel

We publish a wide range of titles, including general interest publications, guides to individual towns, and books for outdoor activities centred on walking and cycling in the great outdoors throughout England and Wales. This is a recent selection:

General interest:

THE INCREDIBLY BIASED BEER GUIDE – Ruth Herman
This is the most comprehensive guide to Britain's smaller breweries and the pubs where you can sample their products. Produced with the collaboration of the Small Independent Brewers' Association and including a half-price subscription to The Beer Lovers' Club. *£6.95*

DIAL 999 – EMERGENCY SERVICES IN ACTION – John Creighton
Re-live the excitement as fire engines rush to disasters. See dramatic rescues on land and sea. Read how the professionals keep a clear head and swing into action. *£9.95*

THE ALABAMA AFFAIR – David Hollett
This is an account of Britain's rôle in the American Civil War. Read how Merseyside dockyards supplied ships for the Confederate navy, thereby supporting the slave trade. The *Alabama* was the most famous of the 'Laird Rams', and was chased half-way across the world before being sunk ignominiously. *£9.95*

PEAK DISTRICT DIARY – Roger Redfern
An evocative book, celebrating the glorious countryside of the Peak District. The book is based on Roger's popular column in *The Guardian* newspaper and is profusely illustrated with stunning photographs. *£6.95*

I REMAIN, YOUR SON JACK – J. C. Morten (edited by Sheila Morten)
A collection of almost 200 letters, as featured on BBC TV, telling the moving story of a young soldier in the First World War. Profusely illustrated with contemporary photographs. *£8.95*

FORGOTTEN DIVISIONS – John Fox
A unique account of the 1914 – 18 War, drawing on the experience of soldiers and civilians, from a Lancashire town and a Rhineland village. The book is well illustrated and contains many unique photographs. *£9.95*

ROAD SENSE – Doug Holland
A book for drivers with some experience, preparing them for an advanced driving test. The book introduces a recommended system of car control, based on that developed by the Police Driving School. Doug Holland is a highly qualified driving instructor, working with RoSPA. *£5.95*

Books of Walks:

RAMBLES IN NORTH WALES
– Roger Redfern

HERITAGE WALKS IN THE PEAK DISTRICT
– Clive Price

EAST CHESHIRE WALKS
– Graham Beech

WEST CHESHIRE WALKS
– Jen Darling

WEST PENNINE WALKS
– Mike Cresswell

STAFFORDSHIRE WALKS
– Les Lumsdon

NEWARK AND SHERWOOD RAMBLES
– Malcolm McKenzie

NORTH NOTTINGHAMSHIRE RAMBLES
– MAlcolm McKenzie

RAMBLES AROUND NOTTINGHAM & DERBY
– Keith Taylor

RAMBLES AROUND MANCHESTER
– Mike Cresswell

WESTERN LAKELAND RAMBLES
– Gordon Brown

WELSH WALKS:
Dolgellau and the Cambrian Coast
– Laurence Main and Morag Perrott *(£5.95)*

WELSH WALKS:
Aberystwyth and District
– Laurence Main and Morag Perrott *(£5.95)*

MOSTLY DOWNHILL:
Leisurely walks in the Lake District
– Alan Pears

WEST PENNINE WALKS
– Mike Cresswell

CHALLENGING WALKS IN NORTH-WEST BRITAIN
– Ron Astley *(£9.95)*

WALKING PEAKLAND TRACKWAYS
– Mike Cresswell *(£7.95)*

– all of the above books are currently £6.95 each (except where noted)

LONG-DISTANCE WALKS:

THE GREATER MANCHESTER BOUNDARY WALK
– Graham Phythian

THE THIRLMERE WAY
– Tim Cappelli

THE FURNESS TRAIL
– Tim Cappelli

THE MARCHES WAY
– Les Lumsdon

THE TWO ROSES WAY
– Peter Billington, Eric Slater, Bill Greenwood and Clive Edwards

THE RED ROSE WALK
– Tom Schofield

FROM WHARFEDALE TO WESTMORLAND:
Historical walks through the Yorkshire Dales
– Aline Watson

THE WEST YORKSHIRE WAY
– Nicholas Parrott

– all £6.95 each